THE

SECOND
PHILOSOPHY®

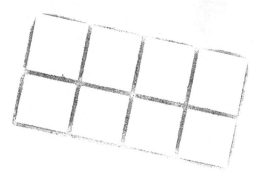

THE

SECOND PHILOSOPHY®

A Practical Guide to Releasing Your Inner Genius

DEREK MILLS
THE STANDARDS GUY®

HAY HOUSE

Australia • Canada • Hong Kong • India
South Africa • United Kingdom • United States

First published and distributed in the United Kingdom by:
Hay House UK Ltd, 292B Kensal Rd, London W10 5BE.
Tel.: (44) 20 8962 1230; Fax: (44) 20 8962 1239. www.hayhouse.co.uk

Published and distributed in the United States of America by:
Hay House, Inc., PO Box 5100, Carlsbad, CA 92018-5100.
Tel.: (1) 760 431 7695 or (800) 654 5126; Fax: (1) 760 431 6948 or (800) 650 5115.
www.hayhouse.com

Published and distributed in Australia by:
Hay House Australia Ltd, 18/36 Ralph St, Alexandria NSW 2015.
Tel.: (61) 2 9669 4299; Fax: (61) 2 9669 4144.
www.hayhouse.com.au

Published and distributed in the Republic of South Africa by:
Hay House SA (Pty), Ltd, PO Box 990, Witkoppen 2068. Tel./Fax: (27) 11 467 8904.
www.hayhouse.co.za

Published and distributed in India by:
Hay House Publishers India, Muskaan Complex, Plot No.3, B-2, Vasant Kunj,
New Delhi – 110 070. Tel.: (91) 11 4176 1620; Fax: (91) 11 4176 1630.
www.hayhouse.co.in

Distributed in Canada by:
Raincoast, 9050 Shaughnessy St, Vancouver, BC V6P 6E5.
Tel.: (1) 604 323 7100; Fax: (1) 604 323 2600

A catalogue record for this book is available from the British Library.

ISBN 978-1-84850-978-8

Printed and bound in Great Britain by TJ International, Padstow, Cornwall

This book is dedicated to those people who I love and respect the most:

My wife, Gerry;
she is as much a part of me as I am;

To my children, Sebastian, Rochelle, Yasmin, and Dominique, who have taught me so much;

To my father, who kept my world together when I was 13 years old and my mother passed away;

To my mother, whose love and affection I still feel and remember;

To my brothers and sisters, Pansy, Maxine, Floyd, Doreen, Paul, and Lee, who have given me the joy of unconditional love, all of my life.

Contents

Acknowledgments

I would like to thank my family and friends for the time that they gave me to write this book. My gratitude to Ruth Needham, my confidante and literary agent who has constantly held a space for me, assisting me on my journey. Also I would like to thank all the friends who have helped me on my journey, including Michael Brown, Peter and Sara-Beth Roper, Farah Pandith, Sonja Graham, Deborah Price, Charles Barwell, Sheila Holt, Sue McLeod, Sandy Draper, and the Hay House team.

The Reluctant Guru

For a while I considered myself to be a reluctant 'guru.' Not because I didn't want to help others find their inner wisdom and happiness, but because initially I had no more idea than a goat what specifically I was 'doing' that was helping people. I was living it and I was just excited by its impact on others. But people were asking me questions, and treating me like a guru when I answered. They connected with me. The one thing that most people consistently say is, 'Derek's got a "certain something."' What I discovered was that if I have, then so does everyone else! Even in the early days when, like me, they didn't realize what that 'something' was, they just felt it and began to ask questions.

I noticed that if we pause and go a little deeper within ourselves, we can *all* release that inner 'something.' People came to me, first one at a time, then in tens, then in thousands. The reason they sought me out was because I'd turned my life around from failure and despair to happiness and phenomenal success. People were asking how I did what I did, and how I got myself from where I was to where I am. The more they asked, the more I had to go inside myself to discover more of the 'something.' I found I was able to access more of myself and help find the answers for them to such a profound level that I was able to change their lives and continue to change mine. Further, it was the realization that as we all had that 'something' inside us, the question became, 'How can we uncover and release it?'

My life is like one of those classic before-and-after shots. From the night that I experienced my '10-second moment,' I found my voice and was able to articulate better, to speak with confidence, clarity, and certainty on matters I had struggled with before. People approached me for advice, guidance, and insights based upon my philosophy, which I now call the 10-Second Philosophy® because that's the amount of time it took me to change.

I know many of them came to me at first because of the difference they saw in my business and sales results, but quickly they realized that there was 'something else' going on inside that brought success outside. I gave freely, because I had changed and was able to share wisdom and insights in ways that people understood. In that time, I constantly heard friends, associates, and professional speakers make comments such as:

'I've never heard it that way before.'
'I get it now.'
'I would love to connect with you.'

'It's brilliant!'

'Refreshing, I never saw or thought about it that way before.'

'This is something I can go and use right now in parts of my life.'

'I've used all of the positive mental attitude stuff, this is different.'

'I've set goals all of my life, and I'm still not happy and successful! There's an alternative?'

'I like the idea of using Standards now.'

'I can use this stuff.'

Life coaches asked, 'How have we been missing this? It's so obvious when you hear it.' Some people shared with me the fact that my 'something' had a resonance or an internal familiarity with them; that they got it and knew immediately what it meant to them once they heard the message. Others didn't say a thing, they just internalized the idea, and later I would get handwritten notes, e-mails, and SMS texts as the effect of what the philosophy meant for them sunk in. For the left-brain, logical thinkers out there, I will add that there's a huge bottom-line effect to this stuff if you want to become wealthy and successful.

I realized I'd been living and creating a philosophy, and people were seeking me to help them get what was important to them. In this process my gifts and talents flooded out, and that flow continues today as more of my 'Truth' is revealed. The last few years have shown me that it's not just me. The 10-Second Philosophy is a practical approach that starts today and continues. I never intended to be a guru, but I now know that you, I, all of us have 'something,' and I know how to help you uncover it.

⏱ *There's 'something' about you...*

RELEASING YOUR 'SOMETHING'

Failure-to-success stories – we love them because they give us hope. Hope that we can make that 'Journey,' too. But we want more than just the story, what we really want is to figure out 'how.' How did this person do it? What did this person do differently that allowed him or her to succeed, and can I learn it too?

The answers to these questions are in the 10-Second Philosophy, and it will serve you if you're 'failing' in your life. It will serve you if you simply want to improve the quality of your life or discover your 'Faculty,' your inner genius or true calling, as I continue to find mine.

This is the story of how I turned my life around from failure to success and what I learned. What I realized is that change can happen in seconds, in just 10 seconds in fact. After years of setting goals, my breakthrough was waking up to the fact that goals don't work for most people. In that moment what came through to me from my inner self was an intense message that I was failing to be happy and successful after years of goal-setting and that I should instead, from that moment onward, set new, very high daily 'Standards' in all areas of my life, as an alternative way to get results.

For the purpose of this philosophy, a 'Standard' is defined as a *level, rule, quality, criteria, or basis adhered to daily.*

When I set Standards my life truly changed like never before. Since my transformation I have witnessed similar success in the many people I coach and mentor. I'll share their stories with you, and along the way give you the tools, philosophy, and procedures to enable you to see and set Standards in what identifiably are the key areas in your life right now. In my moment I found the real 'me,' my Truth, which I call 'TrueSelf.' It guided me to set Standards and enabled me to unlock a place deep inside that continues to bring forth abundance. I'm going to help you find that place in you and start your Journey to TrueSelf.

And once you start, it doesn't stop, because I've found that this philosophy isn't stagnant. You don't take 1,000 steps and reach enlightenment. It's a living, breathing force, and once you start living from your Truth, your TrueSelf continues to blossom. My Journey is still continuing. Each day I find new resources, set higher Standards, discover more of my inner genius. It's my hope that as you read this book, you'll notice a shift in you. You'll appreciate that your learning is different and increased each time. As you grow and experience, the meaning and message of things will change for you. This is something you *can* do. This book has a message: Change is simple, and you'll see why, shortly.

The beginning of the 21st century isn't just about financial crisis, it's about personal crisis and the opportunity that comes with crisis as it was for me. It's the opportunity for a personal revolution.

10-SECOND MOMENTS AS AN AGENT OF CHANGE

When you find yourself in the middle of your life and realize in a moment that you're not who you're supposed to be, how do you get from the person you've become back to 'You'? You may have lost a job, suffered stress, lost a home, or lost hope. You may feel just plain lost as a result of all the confusion and the 'shift' – for as sure as night follows day there has been a shift. Remember the epoch. If you've been affected, this philosophy is about accessing your greater resourceful self.

The 10-Second Philosophy is about immediate change and revealing your TrueSelf, your inner genius. The right word, thought, question, phrase, or idea is all it takes to cause you to stop, go deeper inside, and reach your TrueSelf. When you live from 'who' you really are and use Standards to keep you in your Truth, life will never be the same again.

My moment came in 2003 when I was at absolutely rock bottom, financially, spiritually, and mentally. From that moment, between 2003–7, and afterward during the world's worst financial crisis for 100 years, I turned my life around so astoundingly that along the way people were asking me how I did it, how my life had just got better and better in all areas, doing things, meeting people, and having opportunities of which I'd only ever dreamed.

In that time, I followed the same business model as before, yet found that more people listened to me. More quality clients took my advice. Millionaires and multi-millionaires wanted my advice and to do business. That success continues today. After four years my new business gross income had increased by more than 10 times. I started doing levels of business that put me at the 'Top of the Table and Court of the Table' in the most internationally recognized professional body for financial planners and wealth managers in the world, The Million Dollar Round Table. In the company I represented, I moved up the agent new-business-results league tables from about #1,000 of 1,200 agents in 2003 to #28 of 1,400 by 2007, and I did it working less than half the time.

During that time, and since, my greatest gifts and talents have flooded out with spectacular results. They have lifted and carried me, and haven't ceased from that one moment. I discovered talents that I didn't know I had and knowledge that wasn't in my conscious mind. In discovering my TrueSelf, my inner genius was awakened. I realized 'I' was the solution to all my previous problems.

⏱ *Live life as your TrueSelf every day.*

A NEW VANGUARD

One of my biggest moments of realization about 'how I was doing it' and my 'something' came in 2008 when I attended an international business program for entrepreneurs, where delegates were given tools, processes, and methods to improve their businesses. My business had expanded so dramatically I thought I needed advice and coaching in order to manage the success and increased volume of work. However, I found that the other delegates, even senior coaches, entrepreneurs, and financial advisers, were asking me questions about my thoughts. As I shared my take on various established business methods, neurolinguistic programming (NLP), quantum physics, and other tools for change and awareness, I realized that I had my own unique approach and people wanted to know more. Something in them made them come to me for answers. They could see I had 'something,' and wanted me to help them find their 'something' too. They wanted to know how to turn their businesses and their lives around. How could they get better results in less time? How could they be more effective and have more time with their loved ones? How could they be healthier? How could they be and feel happier? They asked me because they saw and heard I was doing it.

My answers to their questions made me realize that it wasn't about business models. The practical material on the course could and would work, but it wasn't about the things you did outside; it was about what you did inside yourself that allowed the material to work. Most people can't get themselves to start, follow through, or to properly complete, programs and business systems that would ensure them success. If it were as simple as just following a business model or system, then everyone would just do that and be a success. I left the program.

I continued to define my 'stuff' by sharing it with speakers, influencers, and leaders, and they too said that I had 'something.' So I continued to question, 'What specifically have I got?' Once, I was in an international conference in Los Angeles having a discussion with a senior member of the US government. He suddenly asked me to stop speaking for a moment, took out his notebook, and started writing down what I was saying because he said it would really help him!

I now have a strong internal frame of reference about my 'something,' but back then I wanted to check it out externally, and I went further afield to people who were specialists in the area of personal development and tested it with and in front of them. One of the first things I did was a showcase at a Professional Speakers Association (PSA) chapter meeting. I thought all these people would have heard all the speakers and philosophies so I wanted to make sure my message was unique and usable. It was.

I then tested it in front of an international audience of top professional speakers at the Global Speakers Summit. The response was so positively beyond what I could have imagined that I realized I really was onto something! I had a new vanguard to help people like you, like me, to become our best. It's all right to have something inside you for you, but when the world is calling, you have to share it!

🕐 **This is a life journey not a three-day program.**

A PERSONAL, SPIRITUAL, AND BUSINESS REVOLUTION

During this process I noticed something remarkable – there was a theme. These men and women (who were approaching me for guidance) thought they knew how things were and how they worked, and what was real, and then they found out they didn't. They began to ask me questions such as: 'If this is the case, then who am I really?' and 'How did I get here?' Then they began to play with the ideas: 'What if I'm meant to be doing something else?' and 'How can I do what I've always really wanted to do?' and 'How come I'm not really happy on the inside?' and 'What does it take for me to be happy?' These were telling times, and something inside of them was telling them that there was more to them than they had previously allowed themselves to consider; that 'something' was nudging them. 'Is it time for a change?' they asked. 'Change has already come,' I replied. I knew it, and they knew it, too.

Some of these men and women played with the idea and gave it life and breath. Others allowed it to wither on the vine; they resolved to never travel the road and discover who they *really* were, and what might have been if the real them was in the world. Each had their moment; some of them had more than one moment, and it passed them by. Others grabbed one of their moments, and let it lead and change them. It takes just moments, less than 10 seconds, to realize that you're in 'a moment.' How much of your life are you missing as you rush by the moments that could change you for good?

Recognizing your moments is just the first part, next you need to ask, 'What do I do with them? What is it really? What is its purpose, and how can I capture, benefit, and grow from it? Where could this moment lead me? What can I learn about my TrueSelf that I don't already know?' It's about learning more than you think you already know. I believe that the American author and social commentator Eric Hoffer grasped this point of learning when he said: 'In a time of drastic change it is the learners who inherit the future. The learned [those that think they know how and what everything is already] usually find themselves equipped to live in a world that no longer exists.'

⏱ **Problems are an opportunity to know 'You' better.**

THE WAY FORWARD

Your TrueSelf is your true being and essence. It's also far more because it causes you to be habitually in your Faculty, usually described as being in the 'flow' or 'zone,' and opens up a channel or 'Conduit' to greater intelligence through the Law of Connection. You already know that you are more. Your TrueSelf is the *more* you know. When you follow the path of your TrueSelf, your inner genius and your power are released, and you begin to live and experience your existence at a higher level. Success and happiness are the natural outgrowth of being more in your TrueSelf. From TrueSelf everything else flows.

Your TrueSelf has four characteristics, which are the ways your TrueSelf expresses and reveals itself to, for, in, and through you, and you can use them to serve you and others. We'll explore each of the four characteristics in more detail in Part I, but for now they are:

- **Truth**: The real you living your life, so your happiness increases and you shine honestly for yourself and open up a way for others. Living your life as you.

- **Journey**: As you get to know yourself increasingly well and grow into your TrueSelf, the world 'sees' you differently, too.

- **Faculty**: The best of you is accessed. Your inner genius is more fully enabled.

- **Conduit:** Opens your access to intelligent energy and universal knowledge.

My inner genius gave me Standards at the start of my Journey – I'm known as The Standards Guy® – and from that place my creativity continues to flow. What will yours be? Setting Standards from your TrueSelf is key because it's *what* and *how* you are, and how you live every single day that determines your success. It's how you interact with yourself and others that brings contentment and well-being. A process of setting and living by daily

Standards allows you to always feel comfortable in your own skin, every single day, and that helps determine how happy you are inside each day.

Throughout this book you'll find stories of the shift that happens when you find your TrueSelf, which now I'm now certain you will. Words, thoughts, questions, phrases, and ideas serve as triggers to your TrueSelf, and you'll find they are everywhere. Capture them, because they can create 'moments' for you.

In this spirit, I've included the words, thoughts, questions, phrases, and ideas that resonated with *me* on my Journey to TrueSelf 'everywhere' in this book, marked by a ⏱ symbol. If any of them resonate with you, internalize and meditate on them or use them as mini mantras. Together with the '0–10 Your Moments' exercises, they are designed to put you on the path to help you uncover more of yourself. And if *any* of the ideas in this book cause you to think or feel differently, note it down in your journal, along with the 'moments' of your 'Journey.' If for any reason you don't keep a journal, in the years to come you may regret not capturing what could be the biggest shifts in your personal and business life.

In telling my story my biggest hope is that you capture and create '10-second moments' of your own, and the story you will want to tell begins.

⏱ *Have fun, play with the 'stuff.'*

PART I

AWAKENING

*Most people are not happy because they are not who they truly are. You cannot be **truly** happy as not you.*

Chapter 1

10-Second Wake-up Call

As I was driving home one night, I grew impatient with the driver in front. Exhausted and eager to get home and see my family, I decided to overtake. I indicated, pulled out, and put my foot down. Within a second I felt and heard an enormous crash and buckling sound as my car bounced off the crash barrier and across the lanes of traffic. In my tired state, I had failed to realize that I was already in the fast lane! If there had been a Mack Truck behind me I probably wouldn't be at this keyboard now.

Many of the events in my life have had a profound effect on me. However, it took me a while to realize that God, nature, and the universe were sending me bigger and bigger messages to 'WAKE UP,' but I just wasn't listening. The late nights at work, borderline depression, empty pockets, and my near-death experience on the road that night – not to mention a life balance that didn't factor in being the father of four children and having a wife who needed more than just a pay check – just weren't enough for me to wake up and say, 'Enough!' But shortly after this event my 'moment' came, and I listened and woke up.

⏱ *10-second moments are everywhere,*
watch for them.

GET ON YOUR PATH

Before my moment came I was searching... searching for the path. 'After all, life is a Journey, so follow your path' people tell you. What they don't tell you is how to get to *your* path. It took just 10 seconds to change my life – although it took 18 years or more for me to realize that change was needed – and it came with plans and guidance that I'll share with you in more detail in later chapters. Those 10 seconds didn't just take me along the path, those 10 seconds took me to *my* path. Those 10 seconds took me to my TrueSelf.

0–10 YOUR MOMENTS
· ·

When we hear or see or feel the right word, thought, question, phrase, or idea, it causes us to pause and go inside ourselves, to experience our 'self' introspectively, connecting with who we really are at our core. Then it is about trusting and following the guidance that comes from that inner place.

This is the essence of the 10-Second Philosophy, and it's worth reading again and again until you grasp the wonderful, life-changing possibilities imbued in its simple message. When you become centered and connect to whatever feeling, thoughts, or ideas come from that place you are in TrueSelf. If you then have the courage to follow, act upon, and be guided by whatever messages come from that place, you are living from your TrueSelf and therefore your inner genius. Your inner genius has access to your greatest abilities, talents, and gifts, even those latent or dormant through lack of use.

0–10 YOUR MOMENTS

The questions you may want to ask yourself now are: 'How *could* my success and happiness be now, if I were living more of my life from my TrueSelf' and 'What would life look like in a year, a month, a week, today if I were living it from my inner genius?'

The 10-Second Philosophy exists as an agent of change to let you know that change can happen in an instant and the shift will surprise you. You won't become a billionaire, or your country's greatest ever leader or businessman or woman in 10 seconds. But you will have stepped onto the path that could make all of that happen – and anything else that you desire possible. The 10 seconds that you take – to allow words, thoughts, questions, phrases, or ideas to access your TrueSelf – will get you onto the right path to and for 'You.' It is from that path you become who you truly are, manifest in the world, living the best life you can. Living from your inner genius can't fail to make for you a greater life precisely because it will be the best 'You,' on the right path. If you're already a millionaire or a billionaire you'll know that, although it's a big thing, money isn't the only factor. Getting to your path is the purpose of the 10-Second Philosophy. From there your TrueSelf power will allow you to experience your world around you the way you were meant to.

I've seen and met men and women who have gone from ordinary to extraordinary – which is nothing more than an expression of their TrueSelf – in incredibly short periods of time. You can become the most amazing parent, partner, spouse, salesperson, or creator when you live your life as your TrueSelf. Living your life as 'NonSelf,' as I call it, just won't work. You may be noticing this already. In the quiet space that you go to, when it's just you and yourself, you know this to be true. Resolve now to become great if you're failing. Go from good to great if you are dissatisfied. Commit to find gifts and talents that may well revolutionize your industry, your career, and your life.

So let me share with you how I became happy.

A 10-SECOND REVOLUTION

As I sit here today my joy is that my family and I spend so much time together. We know that we can do what we want with our time. Life is good for us and we enjoy a life of affluence and ease. Each of us has our own lives, but we're part of the whole now. This has been the case for me, my wife Gerry, and the children *only* since the end of 2003 – before then things were very different. There was a long time when I felt frustrated and fearful at every turn and missed out on precious time with my family.

Perhaps it's because of the years I spent away from them, mentally and physically, that even when they or I are being irritable, frustrated, or angry, or just not getting on, my family still thrills me. They are amazing and I love them more than life itself. We vacation, we play, we laugh, we drive together, and sometimes they even laugh at my jokes. We face challenges too, but even those tougher times are, to me, a sign of our lives together, and so they serve to heal the wounds of the past times spent apart. My wife, my children, my brothers and sisters, my father, my aunts and uncles, my nephews and nieces, and my cousins: It's a joy and a wonder to be around them.

Over the years I had my 'moments' and failed to embrace them, until a question from the most unlikely of sources did for me what the 'goal-setting' experts couldn't. It was the utilization of this particular 10-second moment that set me on a path that allowed me to positively impact the lives of people all over the world. Until that moment came, I was so unhappy and unfulfilled, there was no longer any choice.

And then the day came,
when the risk
to remain tight in a bud
was more painful
than the risk
it took
to Blossom.
ANAÏS NIN, *RISK*

I FAKED IT AND DIDN'T MAKE IT

When I was 21, I didn't set out thinking, 'I'll spend the next 20 years failing to meet my goals.' Pretty much like everyone else I set out looking for the good life. I worked on a self-employed, commission-only basis in the financial services industry. By my mid-20s, I'd married Gerry and we'd had our first two children, Sebastian and Rochelle. This was a tough period financially, and we struggled because business was poor, very poor. It was a boom-and-bust economy in which I was always behind the curve, out of sync, never actually booming, but feeling the busts full on. My after-tax earnings were spent just paying the bills. We were living from month to month. Many times the money ran out before the month's end, and twice I saved my house from foreclosure.

In my 30s things just got worse. I was still failing, and for a while I generated less new business income than I had years earlier. Our second and third daughters, Yasmin and Dominique, were born. More mouths to feed – albeit adorable ones. As the sole income generator I was just keeping our heads above water. The stress was having a severe effect on my health. I had pains and imaginary ailments, and was always going to the doctor to be told nothing was wrong. Mentally, it was tough. I don't think I was depressed, but I was 'clinically unhappy'! My financial services performance was so bad that I was near the bottom of the list of the company's 1,200 agents. Twice I tried to leave the industry in an attempt to make a better life, but something inside me wouldn't let me make the leap. So I stayed, unhappy.

In those years I was at the beck and call of some of my clients. They would call and I would go and see them, any time, any place, anywhere. I gave great value, service, and – above all – time to my clients over many years, but they generated very little income for me because most were low income themselves. I never got wealthy clients. Most would only see me at night, which was convenient for them, tough on me. Oh, and one more thing, I was lonely. In the main I was living a fake life, as not-me. When you live life not being true to yourself, as your NonSelf, you will never really make a success of life.

One evening, in November 2003, I was in the office just after 9:30 p.m. The building security guard popped his head around the door and asked me if I was ready to leave, I said I wasn't and needed 10 more minutes. After a while the guard came back. I didn't speak but without looking up used my fingers to motion I needed two more minutes.

Then he asked a rather innocuous question: 'What time did you get in this morning?'

'8 a.m.,' I answered.

He looked at me for a moment before walking away, but the words hung in the air. I internalized his question and my response. Now I know why, because things were so bad, that I was ready for that question. I realized at a deeper level than ever before that my life was shockingly poor in all areas because the life I was living wasn't really me.

'Enough!'

In those next 10 seconds, I looked introspectively. I felt a surge of feelings rise up inside me. I was rooted to the spot yet completely relaxed and felt real balance. As

I stood there, my emotions and energy weren't logical. I didn't have to think about them. I didn't construct them, they came through and to me pure; a pure, incredible knowing with a sense of calm certainty. Even then I knew I was in a different place, so I stayed in that space and kept that moment. In those seconds, looking honestly and deeply within, I knew that if I was going to continue one more day on this planet, it would be on my terms. I would live the life that I wanted. I would be me and not what society, the industry, the media, the recession, my education, my history, and the wrong clients would have me be. I stood there and more was revealed. I always thought that the answers were outside of me, yet in that moment I realized that my current life was intolerable, and there was nowhere else to go but inside. In a moment of clarity I was able to reassess my whole life incredibly quickly, because the real me, my TrueSelf, was speaking to me. I paid attention and my life changed. In that moment I found freedom.

🕐 *What have you had 'enough' of?*

STANDARDS OF CHANGE – PURE GENIUS

One of the first things that came from my TrueSelf was the huge realization that, although I'd been setting goals for 18 years, here I was a failure on every level that mattered to me – personal and business. The message didn't come like a flutter of butterflies, but like the rush of a hurricane. This was 'knowing' that goals weren't doing it for me. I knew exactly what I had to do. I had to live my life, in my 'now' – not hindered by the past or worried by the future – and stop setting goals. The guidance that came from within me was to set new high daily Standards for my life that were congruent with who I really was on the inside. I knew then with a certainty born of intuition that I would make a better life.

While goals are future-based, Standards are a now, *today* experience, and as such change you immediately. As long as I could remember, when I used goals to achieve success my life was a failure and caused me to be unhappy. This was more than practical enlightenment. I also *knew* that if I lived each day by my new higher Standards, then my life would make room for me because I would be living as my TrueSelf, and this was *the* key.

Immediately, I knew I had to quit working with nearly all of my clients. Right there and then I chose just 15 folders of clients who would suit the real me and I them. After 18 years in the logical left-brained business world I was listening to and following my intuition. I never called my other clients again and arranged to have someone else look after them. I also set a Standard for my working hours. I would take the children to school every day and pick them up a few days a week. I wouldn't work late any night of the week, weekends were for my family, and I'd no longer work on Fridays, so I could spend time with Gerry. I set Standards for the quality of my clients. They must come to my office, be millionaires, and be genuinely nice people who suited me. I thought: 'This is my life, after all, and I will choose who I spend it with, in and out of work.'

These were some of my initial Standards, set as an outgrowth of a simple question. It's easy to set new Standards when you accept what's making you unhappy and how you really want to be. When you allow your TrueSelf to come out and be in the world, you change. When you change, everything changes for you.

⏱ **Notice how fear passes.**

Setting Standards is a sure path to your inner genius, and this is where all your answers are for you. It's from here that you realize who you are.

My life is now 180 degrees different and infinitely better because of paying attention and having faith in 'my moment.' This new way took me to a place where I was able to be 'me,' and with the result that I achieved things far beyond any of my original goals. All the pain I'd suffered was given new medicine, new healing, and enabled me to reenter the world 'new and improved,' or you might say 'original and improved.' It was this very practical approach that was a phenomenon to all who witnessed my rise, and brought this philosophy to life immediately in my everyday personal, business, and financial life. Living your life by daily Standards, which are congruent with your TrueSelf and lived one day at a time, will bring you more happiness and success than any goal program or methodology. In doing this we kick away the wooden leg of excuses.

ONE DAY AT A TIME

You're given your life one day at a time and you create your happiness and success each day, one day at a time. Each of your days is given to you – and to no one else – so it's important to live your life as 'You.'

So far, in more than 25 years of studying myself and other people from all walks of life, I have learned that failure and unhappiness are most common if you fail to be who you really are. No matter what level of success and fame people achieve, if they're not doing it as themselves, they fail. Countless celebrities, movie stars, and musicians seem to have it all, yet they are often in the most artificial world of all, furthest from their true selves. Many of them fall early into their graves – often victims of alcohol or substance abuse – because they can no longer keep up the illusion of themselves. Failure comes to those who live as they think the world would have them *be*. Most of us don't have the added pressures of being famous and nonstop media attention, but how many people fall into the trap of believing that just being themselves isn't good enough? They create an image of themselves for the world – fearing criticism, fearing what others will think or say if they were to be 'just' themselves.

It wasn't always like this. Most of us start out with an idea of who we are, but resign ourselves to living and being as we think the world wants us to live and be. As a result, I hold that most people are not happy because they're not living their lives as their true selves.

13

If you're not yourself you'll always find true happiness avoiding you, as you've avoided yourself. Worse, you aren't able to utilize your true powers and access your abilities and gifts. It is as if, when you're in NonSelf, you're cut off from the inner genius within you – which is within all of us. At times in your life, maybe once or a handful of times, you have stumbled into your TrueSelf. You don't know how you got there, but you recognized that place as being somewhere completely different to your other way of living and capabilities. In that moment, you found skills, talents, words, and abilities far superior to those you can usually access. You called it 'the zone' or you said you were 'in the flow.' You perhaps marked that time and refer back to it, as do others who witnessed it, because you behaved so differently. You might wonder why you can't achieve those fantastic results all the time. How many people – reading these words now – still remember such a moment or moments in the flow or zone?

FIXES COME FROM INSIDE–OUT

Dr. Maxwell Maltz was an American cosmetic surgeon and author of the best-selling book *Psycho-Cybernetics*. Maltz realized that when he physically 'fixed' patients' faces, many of them didn't live happy ever after because when they looked in the mirror they still saw a poor self-image reflected back at them. They *still* saw themselves as ugly or not attractive or not right, and many of them wanted 'fixing' again and again. The vast majority of his patients were already attractive on any scale, but they couldn't 'see' it. Dr. Maltz noticed that once they had taken action to be different internally, whether emotionally or spiritually, they stopped looking to the outside for a 'fix' and realized their success and happiness. In other words, when they took the true path of TrueSelf, which is from the inside-out, they created sustainable peace and happiness in their lives. As the Genevan philosopher, writer, and composer Jean-Jacques Rousseau said, 'No one is happy unless he respects himself.'

Every day you continue to live as NonSelf, your yearning, your reason for 'being,' and the sense that 'something is missing' – or that you're not really living as you know you could – will continue. You can only be truly happy as your TrueSelf. Your life, like mine, will change overnight once you take on board a different philosophy. That's all it takes, a different way of looking at things. From now on you can begin to live your authentic life and then you'll marvel at how easy things become for you. Success and happiness – whatever they mean to you – will be yours. How? When living as your TrueSelf you change, and when you do, everything will change for you.

Positive change in an individual is possible in just seconds.

You're good to go as 'You,' but first I'd like to introduce you to the first of a few friends of mine whom you'll meet in this book. They have all experienced their 'moment' and stepped onto their TrueSelf path and are happier for it, and the world is a greater place because of it. I hope they, by guiding and leading in their own way, will help you find your TrueSelf.

Steve Olsher

As Steve held his dying stepfather's hand he had a flash – a thought that changed him forever. Prior to that moment Steve had spent his life 'building businesses, selling them, sometimes winning, sometimes losing,' and it consumed him. As he held his stepfather's hand he had a vision of his own funeral and eulogy: 'Here lies Steve Olsher, he lived his life chasing the almighty dollar.' In that moment Steve met his TrueSelf coming the other way and turned his life around. His stepfather was unable to speak, but Steve experienced a sense of speaking to him through their physical connection, and took guidance from that place. He immediately set about living his life as his TrueSelf. Steve continues to live as himself and is now a successful leader, award-winning author, teacher, and speaker based in Chicago, Illinois, USA.

Molly Lord

Molly hoped to be selected as a teacher on NASA's space shuttle Challenger. She made it through the first and second rounds, but failed to make it to the final cut and couldn't understand why. 'I was certain that NASA and infinite intelligence had made a huge mistake,' she said. One year later, on January 28, 1986, she watched, with hundreds of millions of others, Challenger explode shortly after takeoff. In that moment she found herself, she connected with her TrueSelf and began to realize her partnership and connection to everything else. She found her faith. Molly is an incredibly authentic communicator and mentor, and now helps people find who they are using music therapy. She calls them her 'one-on-one life support sessions.'

Max Bolka

Max is an internationally renowned success coach. Many of his clients come to him when they're in financial dire straits. He regularly witnesses and helps people who are in danger of losing everything. Max has witnessed firsthand that the greatest difficulties can bring the best opportunities: 'Often when we hit rock bottom there is that small voice waiting for you that says that there is nowhere to go from here but up. It is from that point that those who pay attention to the voice within are able to turn their life around.'

What is keeping you away from your inner genius?

THE CLOCK IS TICKING

We all have moments, great and small, and we can use those moments to bring about massive and simple changes. Resolve to use your gifts and talents by accepting and utilizing the clarity of your 'moments' when they come. How many people do nothing, even when they recognize a moment as something special? Recognizing your TrueSelf isn't enough, because in order to turn your life around – in order to turn your life on – you need to stay in that place and allow it to speak to you, and then take action accordingly. Otherwise it just passes you by as 'one of those moments.'

0–10 YOUR MOMENTS

Right now, if you pause and think, you may be able to recognize the 10-second moments in your life. Perhaps you were at work and something caused you to stop, think, go inside, and wonder about the word, thought, question, phrase, or idea that came to you. At times you'll have acted on whatever came out from that place. At other times you simply carried on as normal. It might have been as simple as a strong urge to sit in one seat or another, or as important as a signal about a potential mate. You may have called it déjà-vu, a fluke, a weird feeling, or an 'intuitive' moment and left it at that, not aware of the power that lay beneath. You may not have realized what was happening – that something inside of you was alerted to, or triggered by, something outside of you.

Ask yourself, 'Why do you suppose that happened? What did I do?' It probably wasn't an everyday occurrence for you, but notice what you did when it happened. Did you decide to change jobs, ask someone to be in your life, or engage with a stranger? Did it cause you to go left instead of the usual right (only to find that left was the perfect decision), change a friendship, say something to your child or spouse, call a client (or not), or use a different sales script or business process intuitively, instead of doing it by the book?

Now that you know the power of these 'moments,' the key from now on is to hold that place and see what else comes from it. What's for sure is that when you take action and follow your TrueSelf, something happens to take your life in a different direction. The key is to learn to feel for those 10-second moments, and then listen to the intuitive guidance that comes from that place. With practice you'll begin to recognize your TrueSelf intuitive voice, then it's a question of having the courage and a strong enough yearning to act upon that intuition. As the Greek philosopher Heraclitus of Ephesus wrote, 'A hidden connection is often stronger than an obvious one.'

0–10 YOUR MOMENTS

If you're not your TrueSelf then you might want to consider what took you away from and – until now – what kept you away from yourself. What did you deliberately, or by neglect, do to stop you from being who you wanted to be? What stopped you from being 'You'?

Triggers to your TrueSelf are everywhere once you have awareness. When your moments come, grasp them. Hold on to them long enough to listen to the guidance that comes from there. With practice you'll find these triggers happen automatically, and continually take you into your inner genius. From your TrueSelf, whatever you are, whatever you can be, you will be.

THE BEST OF YOU IN THE WORLD

How about you? After all, this book is about you. As I alluded to earlier, living in a time when it seems that things are outside your control and can be taken away from you, is a blessing in disguise, because it may have caused you to question your values, to ponder the meaning of your life, and to put more meaning into your life.

No matter what your industry is, you may also have noticed a shift there. It might have caused you to question things, like: 'What else in my life might not be real? What else is there that I thought I was happy with, only to realize, when things changed, that I wasn't? How come I feel so uncomfortable in my skin, even though I'm wealthier than I was 10 or 20 years ago? Who am I really? Why is my sense of centeredness, balance, and happiness so easily affected?' During a recession, some people feel a shift. In times like these I hear more people than usual speak about a shift in what things mean to them. Is this a sign of the times or something more?

If life is tough for you, release the inner genius of your TrueSelf and life will become easier for you. Things that cause you to be stuck will become unstuck.

I know you're ready for some answers because you're here, now. You may have no idea how much has conspired to bring this material and you together, yet here we are. Is it time... time for change? Change has already occurred and will continue to do so. It's the only constant.

0–10 YOUR MOMENTS

Moments work for us when we get them and hold on to them, allowing the moment to take us inside, looking introspectively. Then it is a question of whether we have the courage and faith to follow the wisdom that comes from that place. Knowledge without action is not wisdom. Have you had your 'moment' yet? It can come at any time. Are you ready? What would you change?

🕐 *Become unstuck.*

Chapter 2

Standards of Change

One cold morning my mother handed me a large gray duffle coat belonging to my older brother, Floyd. He'd outgrown it, and my coat had outworn its usefulness. I was told this was my coat from now on. As children we knew our parents were poor and were used to hand-me-downs, but I really disliked that coat and didn't want to wear it. You see, it was a coat a 12-year-old would wear, yet I was only 9, and it was too big for me! My objections were evidently not enough and I wore the coat to school that day. When the other kids saw me in this supersized garment they made fun of me, as I knew they would. The torture lasted a few days, but then I noticed something. They stopped laughing and just accepted me with my oversized coat, with its overlong sleeves and hood so big it flopped to one side. Before long, I got used to the coat too. I began to like it and walked around in it as if it were Superman's cape.

Wearing that coat was just like raising or setting a new Standard for me. It made me feel as if I was instantly 'there.' It affected how I thought about myself and how the world felt and acted toward me; soon, whenever I put on the coat, everything around me was different. Of course I didn't use the coat as a metaphor for Standards back then, but even now when I think back, I remember the feeling – I acted differently and it actually seemed like my abilities and friendships got better. My new-old coat even affected my ability to do my schoolwork. I put on the coat, and it made room for me in the playground, it changed me. My life changed because I stepped into a bigger way of being by the simple act of putting on a new coat. This isn't only acting *as if,* as important as that is, it is actually taking on the mantle of someone (me) with that higher Standard. Eureka!

> ⏱ **When you set high Standards, the world will make space for you.**

COAT ON A HOOK

I didn't know it at the time, but I could have considered that coat rather like a goal. I could have hung it up – on a real or imaginary peg – and then said to myself, 'I'm nine years old, I'll put the coat out there, on this peg, for the future. In time, my goal is to wear it. When I'm big enough, good enough, or great enough then I'll take the coat off the peg and put it on.'

What if I had done that? The coat would have been on the peg and my enhanced life, increased self-esteem and connection with others, my confidence, and my 'Superman feeling' would never have existed.

0–10 YOUR MOMENTS
....

What coat have you got hanging on a hook, waiting until you're big enough or good enough? What have you put out there in your future, waiting to make you happy and successful one day, that you could put on today?

I put on the coat and kept it on, even though it was 'too big' for me in places. When I did that, everything became different as I and everyone around me was forced to look at me differently. Think about your life. When people see you differently, don't they treat you differently? You know that most people command and generate more respect and authority wearing a tuxedo than a swimsuit, but why is that? When you get a promotion or begin a new job or career, don't you do a 'cape-walk' too? This is key: If you feel different, you change how you act, how you project yourself, and how others see you. If you can get your true 'coat' or 'coats' on and walk around in them, the world will treat you differently and make room for your rise.

Setting and sticking to higher Standards is just like putting on and wearing a new coat. In setting higher Standards you step into your true, powerful self now and live from that place, as you really are. I learned and remembered this because when I was nine my mother said, 'Just put on the coat now,' so I put on the coat.

A NEW WAY OF BEING

When I stood in my office that fateful evening I had no idea of the extent of what was being revealed to me; I was at such a low point that I didn't appreciate the significance of what I would go through. In that moment of clarity I had tapped into my TrueSelf because of a question. As I stood there, I knew I'd hit rock bottom and my only choice was to follow the rabbit of new thoughts along the path. In that moment I stood transfixed for only a few seconds, and I knew my old way of being just wasn't working. I knew that the answers lay in my being true to myself, and allowing what came from my core to guide me. As I did this, I felt an overwhelming surge of knowledge and certainty.

What came from within was my TrueSelf's voice telling me to 'STOP SETTING GOALS, and instead set new and higher daily Standards, set new and higher daily Standards, set new and higher daily Standards.' When I felt this, I knew this was my inner-self speaking, it was the real me. After all my trials and tribulations my TrueSelf was finally being heard. You don't have to be splashing around in the water to have an Archimedes moment. A eureka moment can come from the simplest of places.

🕐 *When you change, everything will change for you.*

A Standard is a rule, a quality, basis, level, or criterion you live by each day, which honors and is congruent with the real you inside.

- Standards come from the inside out.

- Setting higher Standards for your daily life will fulfill you.

My eureka moment made so much room for me in my life, my relationships, my business, and in forging a new career. In that moment I was reborn and I knew my gift. What I wrote down in that moment was so different from anything I had written down before because it gave me a new approach to life. After 18 years in business, goals weren't working for me! Here I was, a miserable failure in all the areas of my life that mattered to me: my relationships, my health, my finances, and my peace of mind were only a few.

Right there and then I reviewed all that was dear to me. I intuitively knew I had to set new higher Standards for all areas, because everything, large or small, affects everything else. I stood in my office, grabbed a pen and paper, and began writing out a new way of life. Below are some of the Standards I set for myself in the beginning. I have since learned, refined, and added to this list.

- Work Monday to Thursday. Wednesday is a half-day.

- Take the children to school every morning and then go into the office.

- Pick up the children from school four days a week (and stay at home with them).

- Fridays and weekends are family and me days.

- Meetings with clients are held *only* in the office, and clients come and see me no matter where they are in the country.

- Be open and honest with everyone about how I feel about our relationship, and *if* there is to be one (particularly with clients).

- See clients only two days a week. Other workdays are spent on other aspects of the business.

- All new clients must be millionaires at the minimum.

- I closed the file on 95 percent of my current client bank because they didn't suit my new criteria and me. I never called that 95 percent again, and eventually transferred them to someone else.

- All clients must be friendly, open, and good–at–heart people because I want to enjoy my time with them. It's my life after all. (Other advisers and staff still comment on how congenial my clients are.)

- Work in a peaceful, relaxing atmosphere. (When I set my new Standards, I cleared my office of papers and filing cabinets. Later I organized my office into a relaxed and chilled meeting room with music, quality chocolates, cookies, bone china, and comfortable sofas for my clients. I was the first in the building to adopt this approach of creating a quality client experience. Since then many brokers in the company branch network have followed suit.)

- Include some form of exercise in my day (gym or karate initially).

- Forego my membership of any pity-party 'clubs.'

- Associate exclusively with people who empower me, and who positively affect my growth and journey. I quickly broke rapport with those who didn't honor me. (I also let go of some friends and acquaintances who were taking me in the wrong direction.)

- Keep my thoughts on the things I want and off the things I don't or shouldn't want, because where attention goes, energy flows.

- Control my environment to and from work by playing motivational, educational, inspirational, and empowering music and audio in the car. (An hour-long commute means I will get a 'degree-plus' education in time I had previously wasted. My children are in the car for half of my morning and evening drive, so they will learn consciously and unconsciously, too.)

- Don't watch the news or read negative media. I only take in positive messages from media that I can filter or choose.

- Wear bespoke, dark blue pinstriped suits for business meetings.

COMING HOME AGAIN

When I got home I was buzzing like never before; all my energy, abilities, gifts, and talents were flying in unison. Anyone who's in business, works in a large company, or is a sole trader can set and keep higher Standards that are meaningful to them and their business. Anyone who works in a sales or consultative capacity can stop and change their lives, and their results, to such an extent they will wonder what they were doing before.

Standards made an immediate impact on my personal happiness, my health, my relationships, and my business results. The next day I created and laminated a color-coded timetable that showed the Standards for the new husband and daddy that I now was. I gave a copy to each of my children, and Gerry, and stuck a copy on the refrigerator when I got home that night. If you want to stick to any new Standards that you create, be sure to share them with your children. They will keep you on track better than any adult.

In those moments, when I let my old way of life fall away, my TrueSelf let my new life and the real me fill the void. I had been in pain so long, yet the answers to my true-life joy were short. As I kept to those Standards they continued to make room for me and let my TrueSelf direct me. Over and over again I'm guided to take this or the other path or direction. I pay attention and I take the guidance on board. The guidance is after all coming from the best of me.

I believe that the key idea to come from my TrueSelf was to set new Standards because the old ones weren't working for me. They weren't from me and I had blindly adopted them. My TrueSelf knew this and that is why it took me there first. I don't even know where my old Standards in life came from. Do you know where your current Standards came from? The rules, criteria, quality, basis, and levels by which you run your life and business; did you choose them? If you've had them since you were much younger, do they still serve your career, relationships, and health?

> ⏲ **What about your current**
> **Standards lets you down?**

A GOOD MAN AND TRUE

My greatest all-time sports personality is the boxer and humanitarian Muhammad Ali. In his autobiography, *The Soul of a Butterfly,* he tells the story of how he stood against the war in Vietnam and was stripped of his hard-earned career titles, license, and possessions as a result. Yet he remained true to himself and his Standards and never let others pull his strings. Ali lived one day at a time, and says: 'One of the most important aspects of my spirituality has been gradually recognizing all the moments in my life when God was working though me, inside and outside the ring... At night when I go to bed I ask myself, "If I don't wake up tomorrow, would I be proud of how I lived today?" With that question in mind, I have tried to do as many good deeds as I can, whether it is standing up for my faith, signing an autograph, or simply shaking a person's hand. I'm just trying to make people happy.'

🕐 *BeAllYouCanBe.*

The list of Standards I wrote down that night was just the start. I continue to refine them to suit me as I grow, continually putting on bigger or different 'coats' as more of my TrueSelf is revealed to me. Standards keep me in my TrueSelf space, and when I set new ones they take me back inside even further and I find more of my TrueSelf. Most of my adult life I was lost, off my path; Standards help me find and keep to my path. That's the wonderful benefit of setting Standards, you have to look introspectively in order to set them, and so they take you inside and come from you. When I found myself, I didn't write out a list of goals and now I know why.

🕐 **It's not about the destination,
it's about the Journey.**

STANDARDS VERSUS GOALS: ONE DAY AT A TIME

I always found it frustrating when I had to constantly look to next month; next quarter; or the next one, three, five, or 10 years. Having distant goals can actually be demotivating because they appear like illusions on the horizon. We can't reach them and, because this is where much of our happiness lays, we don't really buy into them. The negative kickback of not achieving your goals is that it affects your self-esteem and your 'now' – how you feel and behave today.

You're probably familiar with the sacred (until now) acronym SMART that all goal-setters must bow down to and which must be followed. SMART stands for:

Specific
Measurable
Achievable
Realistic
Time-related

In my experience, SMART goals often cause people to feel DUMB as a result of using them to achieve success. The acronym DUMB is what some people experience when goals fail to bring them the success they promise. It stands for:

Disillusioned when they haven't worked.
Unmotivated when they don't achieve their goals.
Mad when they see their lives staying the same, year after year.
Bored by the idea of updating or creating new goals.

Life is about the journey, isn't it? God willing, we are long on the journey of our lives, and the actual point of arrival is just a part of that. Isn't it better to travel well and enjoy each and every day, instead of measuring yourself against some external factor that will only give you a continual sense of shortfall? In setting higher Standards, you 'realize' and 'be' yourself daily, one step at a time. In doing this you're able to call on the support of your greatest resources within and other people to keep you in your TrueSelf and 'be all you can be' each and every day. That is how Standards work. They aren't some future-based reality, expectation, or hope (a goal). Instead you operate by your Standards today, just today, one day at a time. Then each day everything begins to collaborate in your favor. When everything is for you, nothing can be against you. If you won the jackpot, you wouldn't necessarily choose to win it aged 97 would you? At that point, it would be about the legacy that you left behind – your values as well as your valuables. What you want is the best of your life today.

Consider the Standards that you live your life by: Did you even choose them? Do they serve you? I have come to recognize Standards as being an accelerant to success and happiness because they help people to access their inner genius. What I have understood since that moment in my office is that goals have a limited ability to affect most people dramatically because they are based mainly on the individual or their organization being, having, or doing something out there in the future and are limited in actually changing the present. Goals actually distort the reality of your present.

THE AGE-OLD PROBLEM WITH GOALS

There is a direct correlation between penalty shoot-outs in soccer and the 'goals' we set ourselves in life. Professional soccer players practice their penalty-taking skills conscientiously, because it should be relatively simple to get the ball past the goalkeeper, and most can do it with their eyes closed, literally! So why, in key moments or games, do they miss? The player can see the ball on the penalty spot, some 12 yards from the goal, he sees his teammates standing nervously on the halfway line, biting their nails or with their hands over their eyes. He feels the anticipation and fear of the crowd in the stadium, and at some level he doubts his ability, even though he can do that very thing extraordinarily well in practice.

In life you are the player in the game on the penalty spot, standing looking at a goal you haven't achieved yet. Your teammates are your family, friends, associates, or colleagues. Even among them, when you set about a business or personal goal, some are with you, while some doubt and fear for you. The stadium crowd is made up of people in the world around you. Some will be behind you and support you, some will be happy if and when you fail. Some will hope that you fail.

The problem is that when you have yet to score your goal, you and all around you know it and act accordingly toward you. This is important. The player on the spot misses the goal because, consciously and unconsciously, they absolutely know they haven't achieved their goal yet (i.e., the goal is over there, but when they do their reality check, the ball is right at their feet). The same is true of your goals – there is always a gap between you and the goal itself, and you know it. This knowledge of the 'gap,' like the soccer player, impacts your very ability to get the best of you in the game.

Have you ever used goals as a pathway to success? When I ask this question of an audience, I pretty much get almost 100 percent of those attending raising their hands in response to my question. Is your hand up?

The next question is: 'Based upon goal-setting over the last one, three, five, 10, 20, or 30 years of your life, who is truly happy and successful using goals, and is achieving everything that they know they can?' A few hands are raised in response. If setting a goal is so effective, how come?

There is a goal-setting tradition across the world. This isn't just a New Year resolution thing; people set goals because, well, we always have. I always ask the question: 'How's that working out for you; are you happy?' Many experts in the field of personal development often state: 'If you have no goals, you're not going anywhere.' I ask: 'What if you were to realize that you were living according to Standards you haven't consciously chosen? You're then going somewhere that you don't even want to go – that you don't even realize you shouldn't be going.' Many paths diverge in the woods ahead, some you shouldn't follow. You might be working now in a career or job, with companions and in a manner you didn't choose. Around you are people pulling you in directions that are okay for them, but not right for you – slowing and weighing you down with their luggage. They don't know your 'Truth,' so it isn't any surprise that they load you up with the wrong things to carry.

0–10 YOUR MOMENTS
. . . .

It's bad enough carrying your own luggage, isn't it? Notice whether you are carrying other people's luggage, too. If your true success and happiness is based in your future, when do you begin the career you've always wanted, when do you start to exercise, when do you reduce your alcohol consumption, when do you treat those around you like gifts, when do you write that book, when will you relax, and when will you allow yourself to live as and be the real you? The answer is that you never live your life as the real 'You' if your life is always out there in the future, on a peg... waiting. Today is all you have. When are you going to begin to act from this Truth?

The real answer to the problem of goals is to set rules, criteria, levels, and qualities as the basis for how you live as you, one day at a time, and not allow these 'Standards' to be breached. Decide these areas and *stick to your Standards*. I'm not saying do this for the rest of your life, just for today, each day, and one day at a time. If we live at, or near, our best Standards by the day, our future todays will be better todays for us and all we hold dear.

Over 2,000 years ago Christ taught 'give us this day,' not this decade, not this month, not this quarter, and not this fiscal year. Give us this day. Somewhere in there, there's a message.

A PERSONAL AND
BUSINESS REVOLUTION

What happened when I set Standards was a revelation to me, and the change came immediately, as my life became classic 'before' and 'after' shots. From that night, even though my actual results hadn't changed yet, I was able to articulate better, to speak with confidence, clarity, and certainty on matters I'd struggled with before. I increasingly felt and acted from a place of centered contentment. I found my voice. I found that people approached me for advice, guidance, and insights. I gave freely, as I realized that something was going on. I had changed and was able to share wisdom and insights in ways that people understood. The more I walk and articulate my Truth, the more people ask about it.

I'm passionate about setting Standards and have seen many others utilize Standards to achieve real success. I'm a spiritual and also a very practical person, so I was overjoyed to learn that positive change in a person's life can happen in just a moment, about 10 seconds. I know that you can pray or meditate as much as you want, but as the American educator Marva Collins said, 'God/ the universe isn't in the habit of dropping meat through the ceiling.' For this to happen, and it does, we must do our part, too. We must set and live proactively by higher Standards. We must get off our knees, tune in, take action, and make use of our connection to all things. Trust in God, and tie up your camels. My close friend Karl George MBE has a saying: 'Most people only try. I make sure.' He lives by Standards now, and his Standards have changed his life and the lives of those he mentors.

> 🕙 *There really is the power of*
> *possibilities within you.*

0–10 YOUR MOMENTS
••••••••••••••••••••••••••

Allow yourself to be centered and present, then simply consider the Standards you have in the seven areas listed below, which I call PERFECT Standards. Hold for now whatever feelings and thoughts come from that core place. This initial process is essentially a Standards 360-degree review of your life and career. This is all you need do for now as you begin to listen out for the intentions of your TrueSelf.

Personal Health and Fitness

Environment (internal attitude and external situations)

Relationships

Family

Emotions

Career

Time

In Part II, you'll find out how to use the PERFECT Life Standards System, but if this idea resonates with you, start writing out your Standards as you read. To borrow the words of the performance coach Jack Black: 'It only works.'

ACCELERATED SUCCESS

Setting Standards causes you to set a level of thought, action, habit, quality, and ideal. Standards cause and compel you to live at the 'cause' rather than at the 'effect' end of the world around you. When you live at cause, you're in charge. When you live at effect, the world controls you and takes you where it wants. Pay attention to all of these areas and more, do it daily, all day, every day. When you live with your new Standards in place you immediately begin to act and see yourself differently, and therefore treat yourself differently. In doing so you automatically produce a bend in the world to treat you differently, too. As a result, you can make changes in the ostensibly big parts of your life, such as your career and relationships.

Even an apparently small Standard can bring about a massive change in your circumstances, while the absence of defined, congruent Standards in parts of your life can keep you down. Don't worry or have any concerns for tomorrow, for tomorrow will make the best of itself if you do the best of yourself now, today. When you live at consciously selected Standards chosen from your TrueSelf, or core (heart and intuition), you actually create a different future for yourself than what might have been.

Belief in yourself is as important as the habit of setting Standards and sticking to them long enough to see what would happen if you did. We've all heard the sage advice 'Believe in yourself.' Probably a well-meaning or significant person in your life noticed that you didn't have the belief in yourself that everyone says you should. But were you ever told how?

Many people find it hard to really believe in themselves. Why is that? Because they don't believe that they *can* believe in themselves because they, well, *don't* believe in themselves. It's a vicious circle. Standards are a practical way out of this conundrum, because setting and living by Standards draws out your personal values. When you work at the deeper level of your values then big changes occur up top. The changes will come and with them your belief. You will be able to sit and watch the universe conspire in your favor. Do the thing and you shall have the power. Or in the words of Dr. Norman Vincent Peale, one of the most influential authors and spiritual leaders of the 20th century: 'Change your thoughts and you change the world.'

⏱ *New standards change your behavior.*

DON'T WAIT ANY LONGER

So what's important to you – your lifestyle, spiritual life, material gains, your contribution to society, your relationships and emotions? The world conspires to treat you at your existing Standards. That's why you are where you are. Adjusting your Standards is like changing the set of your sail. It can take you somewhere else, and quicker!

Long-term personal goals assume you'll be here in the long-term to enjoy the fruits of your labors. What if you're not? Then you would have spent the majority of your life living as NonSelf, only to miss the big prize. There is something inherently wrong with an approach that has you losing all your todays just so you can shout 'bravo' when you hit a goal some day in the future – that's assuming that you do hit it. I prefer to shout 'bravo!' and punch the air daily as an expression of my ongoing daily success and happiness, living as me, at my Standards, as my TrueSelf. Wouldn't you?

> ⏱ *If there was no guarantee of*
> *many tomorrows, what would*
> *you change today?*

Don't wait any longer to live as who you really are and as you truly want to be. Your TrueSelf is the very best of you. It is the very essence of your being and knows you best. Your TrueSelf has immeasurable and phenomenal abilities that are available to you because they are part of you, even though you may have only accessed them a few times in your life, and perhaps dismissed those moments as nothing more than being 'in the zone' or 'in the flow.' As you'll find out in the following chapters – which explore the four characteristics of TrueSelf (Truth, Journey, Faculty, and Conduit) – overlooking your own genius is a hard pill to swallow.

0–10 YOUR MOMENTS

Standards changed every part of my life – immediately. Do you get it? What Standards do you live by? What Standard could you set or raise and see immediate change? Choose one area of your life and set a new higher Standard in that area. Then watch how everything changes as you live by that Standard today, and then one day at a time.

Do you really want to know,
or are you just asking?

10

CHAPTER 3

Truth: It's Not Out There, It's in You

*A few months before that revelatory night in my office –
when I finally listened – I had sat down with a prospective
client, Mr. S., who had an investable portfolio worth
$400,000 (in 2003). At the time it was the biggest case I'd
ever tried to get. Despite being well prepared and giving
a great presentation, I think Mr. S. knew I wasn't ready.
I wasn't fooling anyone – not even myself. I wasn't myself
because I was still stressed, fearful, frustrated, and trying to
be what I thought the world wanted me to be. I was almost
completely in NonSelf. Inside I was just a scared little boy,
without the Superman cape. He could probably smell my
fear, I was so uncomfortable. I felt like a fraud. Needless to
say, I didn't get the business.*

It's easier for other people to be truthful and open with
you if they sense that you are authentic, that you are
congruent. Not surprisingly, therefore, Mr. S. didn't say:
'Hey, Derek, great presentation, but I just sense that if

you're not up to it on the inside, you won't do a great job on the outside. Don't ask me how I know, I just *do*.' Instead he simply said 'No,' and I was none the wiser. Now I can see my NonSelf for what it was, I would have said 'No' too.

⏱ *Right now, there are many other things that you could be doing...*

THE FIRST CHARACTERISTIC OF TRUESELF IS 'TRUTH'

Since the time that I followed my TrueSelf and raised my Standards, I've been able to sit down with a comfortable feeling inside. Since those 10 seconds – when I allowed the security guard's question to open my eyes to the Truth – it's as if, while I couldn't possibly know how well things were going to turn out in my life, I knew that it was going to be good and much closer to my sense of a happy life.

You'll recognize your TrueSelf because it's your heart, your inner child, so it knows how to make you happy. Its innate knowledge of you is far superior to your conscious thoughts of you. When you're in TrueSelf you're living on-purpose, your true purpose, and the path brings daily discoveries. In TrueSelf your best gifts and abilities are available to you because it's who you truly are, and it's infinite to the degree that it releases the genius part of you. If you've ever experienced being in the zone or the flow, then you'll know that it exists for you, too. When you're in TrueSelf you can access those abilities at will. In that place, you have more than you consciously know available to you.

Intuition is the *language* of TrueSelf. You can't measure or weigh it, but it's there. It knows you because it's the greater and real you. That's why it's called your TrueSelf.

When I started living as my TrueSelf my circumstances changed rapidly. Almost a year later I was committed to living life as myself and walking my new Journey. Standards changed me immediately and, compared to a year earlier, I was different and I knew it. I could feel it and so could everyone else. I was doing the same financial services seminars in the same hotel, to essentially the same people. But now they were buying from me and becoming clients in ever-increasing numbers. I was on my way. Then I met Mr. and Mrs. C. and things changed again.

Mr. and Mrs. C.'s investable portfolio was worth $12 million (in 2004). Needless to say it superseded the Mr. S. opportunity of the previous year, but their business was worth more than just the fees it could earn me. One of the things I noticed immediately was that Mrs. C. didn't speak. Although she had been brought to the meeting, she appeared to have been muzzled by Mr. C. Whenever I asked her a question in those first few minutes, she grew more reluctant to answer because Mr. C. would jump in, take over, and speak for her. Just 20 minutes into my 90-minute presentation, he had been rude about his wife and continually spoken over her. In the end, after a few attempts, Mrs. C. gave up trying to answer me. Tightlipped, she simply made grunts and head gestures, pointing in the direction of Mr. C. as if to say, 'Don't bother asking me, ask him, he's not letting me speak!' Sitting there comfortably in my TrueSelf, it took only moments to realize that Mr. C. wasn't a particularly nice guy and, while willing to give me some money to look after, he was arrogant and rude. I knew immediately that if I took him on as a client he would make my life a living hell. What he didn't know was that I had already been through hell, and that I wasn't going back.

At this point, I began to close the folder containing my notes and said, 'Mr. C., based upon what I've heard today, I'm afraid I can't accept you as a client because I can see no basis for us doing business together. I think that it would be in both our best interests if we concluded the meeting now.' I closed my folder fully.

Mr. C. was not happy. He was a large, well-built man, and gave me the 'Don't you know who I am?' speech, but I knew precisely who he was and that I had made the perfect decision for both of us. When I'd seen the couple off the premises and wished them the best, I walked swiftly back to the meeting room, closed the door, and jumped off the ground, punching my fist into the air in celebration of my breakthrough. This was a major and early test of whether I could maintain my Standards and my TrueSelf. I passed.

🕐 *Focus on all you truly are and you will make true and greater progress.*

Things had changed again. I was living life true to myself, not based on money. The funny thing is, even back then, I knew if I continued to live from my TrueSelf that the money would come anyway. And it did in abundance.

Whereas I'd previously spent my life tearing around the country seeing anyone with even the smallest amount of money to put into a policy, on any day of the week or time that suited them, now I was turning away a client worth $12 million because I didn't connect with him. Something so dramatic had shifted inside of me. I had changed, and I felt an increasing level of well-being and happiness.

In the year that followed, I took on several clients worth more than Mr. C. As I did, I knew that I would enjoy those relationships.

0–10 YOUR MOMENTS

You may have one or more Mr. C.s in your life, your business dealings, or relationships. How does that make you feel? Do you feel joy and happiness when you think about or deal with them? If not, be more truthful with yourself. Stop for a few seconds and ask the following questions:

Where and when in life do you really experience yourself living from your Truth?

Which relationships are you most relaxed in?

With which clients and activities?

Where do you feel most 'at home' with yourself and happiest?

Where do you feel least honest and 'at home'?

From these answers, from this place, you can take ownership of your relationships and create a shortcut to success.

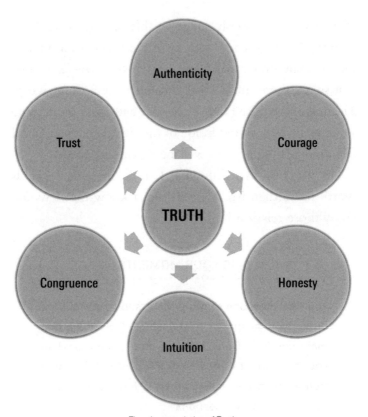

The characteristics of Truth

WHY SETTLE?

When I've shared this episode with other financial professionals, they suggested that I could have referred Mr. C, and still gained financially. What those people didn't understand was that I was experiencing the pure bliss of living from the Truth that called from within me. I no longer care a jot about what I can earn from the clients, and my earnings have multiplied exponentially since sticking to my Standards – my Truth. I have a sense of deep-down knowing, which I trust, about the relationships that are not supposed to be in my life.

When you're in TrueSelf, you come from the perfect place of Truth for you and access your creative, greater intelligence. This is about bringing your inner genius into your everyday world. You too have this practical ability – you've always had it – it's simply about consciously tapping into your TrueSelf and applying its wisdom and intuition.

In just a few short years since I acted on my 'moment' I've gone from being broke, unfulfilled, and unhappy, and scratching around for a living, to:

- Being happy – just being me, and not feeling like I'm trying all the time, just being – and becoming happier every day.

- Spending quality time with my family.

- Being a member of the Million Dollar Round Table (MDRT).

- Meeting many new authentic and amazing friends.

- Speaking, mentoring, and coaching (including multi-millionaires financially) internationally.

- 'Working' when I choose (and because work is a labor of love, I'm not really working, I'm just being me).

- Learning to ride, playing polo, and having my own polo team.

- Co-starring in a personal development movie with some of the world's top life coaches.

- Earning 10 times my original (pre-10-second moment) financial services new business income.

- Loving my life and the positive difference I'm able to make to other people's lives.

So many people don't achieve what they need and want out of life. So many people work every hour possible just to pay the bills. Sacrificing their creativity, their time with their family and friends. Sacrificing themselves. In fact, there are so many people not achieving their goals that there's a need for a paradigm shift. In other words, it's time to look at who you are and how you need to live to feel happier and fulfilled.

This philosophy isn't about taking 1,000 steps or keeping up with others or changing your brand, it's about living your life to Standards that suit you and make you comfortable – it's about being you.

GO MAKE CUPCAKES

When Susan Agony was a child she loved to bake with her mother and grandmother. Then she thought she had to grow up, so she accepted her lot on the treadmill, worked hard, and had a successful career. Until, that is, aged around 50, she rediscovered her TrueSelf and her secret passion. Susan is now a baker and master cupcake maker. Her Sweet and Wicked Cupcake Company makes them oh so well, as my family and I know! This is what Susan does now, yet all of her adult life was spent in the legal profession, regeneration, and international development. A few years ago I met Susan, and she told me that what she'd always wanted to do was bake, even though she'd spent her life as an academic and in the international consultancy arena. This was her passion, and this is now her successful and happy life. She is on her right path. Whatever your inner yearning is, your equivalent of 'making cupcakes,' go do it. Go do 'You' now.

🕐 *Find your something and then be just that.*

THE MEANING OF THINGS AND THE STUFF

Think of your 10-second moments as your TrueSelf tugging on your sleeve, calling you from within in an attempt to get you to 'notice' something or to 'see' someone. More often than not, for most people the challenges and obstacles they face are actually their most significant moments and do their making. The easy times come and go without recognition. I don't know why. I wasn't there when the rules were made.

It seems we begin life as our TrueSelf, then life gets in our way and impacts us in a multitude of conscious and unconscious ways, and we begin to shift into NonSelf. Our TrueSelf often speaks to us or gives us a nudge, but most of the time we ignore it, perhaps telling ourselves 'I can't do that' or 'That's impossible, it's just a childish pipe dream.' Along the way your Truth and true purpose become lost. Along the way we have brief moments –

flashes of who we are and what we're capable of. But as time goes on we pay less and less attention to those moments. We fall asleep to the Truth and refuse to wake up because *things* in the world distract us, with billions of people, bits of information, and everyday problems pulling us away from the Truth – our TrueSelf. To be happy and successful we need to find and live as who we really are; to find our real talents; to grasp our inner greatness, and turn it on. Once you know, NonSelf becomes a choice.

The Aborigines don't have this problem, as they are attuned to their intuition and inner senses in a way that would astound the average city dweller. Hence the majority of our lives aren't spent as we really are, with all our abilities helping us, but as the world has shaped us. The tragedy is that, as a result of this, the world doesn't then get to see and benefit from our true gifts and expression. There is within you a TrueSelf which, if lived, will carry you to your personal greatness. Not being your TrueSelf can be a blueprint for disaster. The discovery of TrueSelf leads to enlightenment.

⏱ **Always have your attention on who you are on the inside.**

There are many *things* that take us away from the real *stuff* of expressing our gifts, our purpose, connectedness, energy, and inner genius. This is the 'stuff' of life. You know you're unique, but do you also know that each of us has a purpose and within us are the gifts and talents for living that purpose? We're often given opportunities to reveal more of ourselves to the world. At other times we unconsciously behave and have traits that don't seem to serve us – this is our NonSelf. Our challenge is to recapture and re-inherit that TrueSelf, to re-inherit that purpose, and to spend the rest of our lives with our inner genius expressed in the world. Only you can live your Truth. The world won't change, but you can look at your world from a different perspective, with a different philosophy; and then, perhaps, you'll find that challenges begin to serve you, and you'll begin to notice that the meaning of things has changed too.

⏱ *Temet nosce (Know thyself).*

We've all been there. Something unexpected or undesirable happens in our lives and in order to move on, we give that episode meaning. We say to ourselves it meant 'x' or it means 'y.' For example, if we lose a job or a lover, we bemoan our lot and say that the loss means we're worthless or unlucky; we allow it to affect our self-confidence and self-esteem. Little do we realize that down the road, the very loss of that job or partner allows us to see things differently, or something else to take its place, which wouldn't have occurred if it weren't for the previous shift. This new twist changes the meaning of the first apparent loss. Then later on, the new opening takes another twist or we're given another closed door or opportunity that changes our lives. We might have the chance to start our own business or to move elsewhere. We know that the business or romantic opportunity wouldn't have been available if we hadn't lost our job or lover, and the event now takes on whatever meaning we ascribe to it. Hence the meaning of the original event has changed. Consequently, we could reason that there are multiple, even infinite, numbers of meanings to everything that occurs, so nothing has any meaning apart from what we attach to it. This is the Tao of meaning.

🕐 *Never let 'things' get in the way of the 'stuff.'*

Over time we change and I'm sure you've noticed how every episode – good or bad – has multiple meanings. As you grow, learn, and change, the meanings of the episode stack up. This tells us that it will have more meanings in the future too. Notice how some things change you and how you change some things. Most of the time we carry our issues around like luggage, for no good reason. This doesn't serve or honor us.

OLD LUGGAGE

I met a young woman who told me that although she had been in her new home for more than five years, she still had boxes and boxes of things in one particular room. She and her husband regularly discussed this and agreed to clear them out, but never did. They kept all the boxes in the room. When I asked her 'How come?' she replied, 'Well I just can't handle that now.' After half a decade of wanting to, she still hadn't got into a place within herself to sort out the things that she knows need sorting. Along the way apathy kicked in, so now she just lives with all those boxes. She doesn't even know what's in most of them, but still they haunt her. Worse still, she needs that room. She plans to make it into a cool, calm, quiet day room. She's had those plans for a while now.

For much of my life I kept a little shop of horrors in my mind. Inside, the shop was full of luggage containing all my bad times, worries, and issues. Over the years I would occasionally take a look inside one of the cases or it would just throw itself onto my path and open itself to me, rather like a flasher in a raincoat. The experience was enough to scare and traumatize me and have me looking around feeling worried for a while after the event – enough to make me question and second-guess myself.

Since I've had the privilege of knowing my TrueSelf, it has served me well in ridding myself of this old luggage. I realized that all my old issues, fears, and worries had one thing in common: They were all unresolved. My TrueSelf would regularly 'throw up' one or more of these issues, and the amazing thing was that within a few seconds I was given the method to solve it. Each issue came with the option of one of three labels:

- Throw away

- Sort away

- Laugh away

And that's exactly what I did. I held a closing-down sale and was free once again. Have you ever been in a situation that is holding you up, but where an older and significantly wiser person knows just what to do? Your TrueSelf knows what you can handle, and when and how.

Throw away

Many of the issues we hold are usually regrets about the past, old limitations, past fears, insecurities, and beliefs. Living in the present meant the past was no longer 'real' to me and couldn't bother me, and I could just throw those issues in the garbage. Things that had been gnawing at me like some deranged gnu for too long. Away, gnu! See yourself throwing (slam dunking if you like) that issue or limitation into the garbage can where it belongs. You might even picture the garbage collection truck taking it away. (That's the furthest I go with that one, but if you want to follow the truck all the way to the furnace, be my guest.)

Sort away

For me this mostly involved other people, but not exclusively. I knew that I had to do my best to resolve them and I did. I was open and honest with those people in a way that cleared the air, or allowed both of us to move on. At times it meant that there was no future communication because the thing that needed sorting was actually an old unspoken truth and served as a door closer on that relationship. Sorting away these problems meant they no longer took up space inside me. From there I was able to travel forward lighter.

Laugh away

You might laugh at some of my past insecurities and fears, or chuckle at some of the things that held me back and say, 'No way, that's such a lame reason to restrict yourself.' Well most of us live in paper prisons of our own making. I broke out of my prison by knowing that the issue was so pathetic that while I couldn't laugh at it yesterday, today I could and did. The very act of knowing I *could* laugh at it made me laugh and empowered me to evaporate it. It's incredible what we sometimes let hold us back, only to wait for time to evaporate it for us. To blazes with time. I'm laughing now and so can you.

Trust your inner genius to know when you can deal with issues that have held you back in the past. As you begin to live as your TrueSelf, so too will come the methods of how to resolve those issues.

0–10 YOUR MOMENTS

Consider any 'boxes' or 'luggage' you're storing. Where might they be? What might they contain? How many of them are there? How do you think you'll feel when you can just throw, sort, or laugh them away? Think about that for a moment. Just for a moment, now. The good news is that you have help. Your TrueSelf is the cavalry. In the very act of recognizing and spending time in your TrueSelf you'll be directed to the best way to resolve them. You'll begin to wonder how you kept hold of those old things for so long.

JUST PART OF YOUR 'STUFF'

This process is part of the TrueSelf process and philosophy. I have been through it and I am still going through it. It is a Journey, and the longer you live as TrueSelf, the fewer issues you'll have in the future. You're on positive ground, life will test your footing and you'll be fine. Continue to let yourself out.

When I lived my life based upon what I thought the world demanded of me, or what it thought I should be, I was lost. When I lived my life based upon who and what I would be, do, or have *in the future*, I became frustrated and confused. My breakthrough came from living in the *now* and being the best, most honest and authentic me in each day. I have found that it's much harder trying to be someone else; it's simpler to be yourself.

Your TrueSelf is there waiting and seeking to express itself, reaching out. It draws your attention to the people, words, phrases, questions, and ideas that will enable you to wake up and pay attention to who you really are and your capabilities.

🕐 *Some things are just so.*

LIVING AS YOUR AUTHENTIC SELF

A lady I mentor said to me early in our working relationship, 'I've previously been scared to be "me" because it felt selfish. Is being me too selfish? I want people to like me.' I've heard similar comments many times. She felt that she had to act in a way that made people like her, but she wasn't happy. The people in her life were 'liking' the person that she knew she wasn't. She was confused and always felt as if she was an 'imposter.' She wasn't being herself. In many of her 'friendships' one party was clearly being deceived, and the other wasn't happy playing the deceiver. No malice was intended, but the game had been going on for many years. This is a trick of NonSelf, and a deception that can last a lifetime.

This is a challenge, isn't it? We all accommodate other people in our lives. That's what it takes to be a happy and contented human being. The problem is that most people take this too far, too early in life, and for too long. They end up living their life for their employer, friend, dad, sister, society, and so on. Have you ever lived and changed yourself for someone or some job that isn't even in your life right now?

When you see the Truth and begin your Journey to your TrueSelf right now, or in just moments, the world begins to see you differently. Some of the world will in fact 'see' you for the first time. The natural result of this is that the world will treat you differently.

TIME TO SHINE

One of the most rewarding outcomes of being your TrueSelf is that everyone who shares your life gets to see more of the real you. There's such magic and greatness and love inside each of us, but somehow it gets lost. This means that when we find ourselves once more, it's actually to the benefit of all of our relationships. Our abilities get the chance to shine without being stifled, embarrassed, restricted, and conformed, which means we quite literally get the best of us into the world. Now you don't have to be Einstein to figure out the potential benefits to you, your loved ones, and your career when you get the best of you out there.

When you're the real you it isn't just your greatest gifts that get to come out and play. There is a special reward for you as you can live mindful of who and what you are in a centered and balanced way. Being mindful means focusing on this present moment in time – your NOW – and not being distracted by what happened yesterday or will happen tomorrow. Experiencing life in the present brings a state of contented awareness that you might also call peace. Being at peace with yourself – not second-guessing yourself because you know how to *be* – mindful of your Truth, your inner place and of others. Being mindful of others means you are infinitely more connected with them, and they with you, and that feeling develops a very creative environment. When you live mindfully of yourself and others you create or 'hold a space' for them that they can just step into when they're with you, because your energy and intention acts as a facilitator for them.

In other words, when you shine in the present you directly and indirectly give 'permission' for others around you to shine too. This is a conscious and an unconscious exchange. When you're mindful of the present moment you're also able to focus on the other person. Your mind is free to relish every moment. You know how you feel when you're around others that are 'just' themselves and 'present,' because you feel comfortable and connected to them. They are great at being themselves – not selfish but selfless. There are no layers to negotiate or see through, they're just who they really are. We all feel better around these people. When we're around them, they allow us to be a little more of ourselves, without all the games, the one-upmanship, the comparisons, the insecurities, or fear of being seen.

My children don't laugh at *all* my jokes – other people's dads are always funnier, aren't they? But, because I'm my TrueSelf, I just keep making those unfunny funnies, because that's me. The real me is 'in the game' with my family, my clients, my friends, and with complete strangers. TrueSelf is about removing the artificial layers and allowing yourself to shine as you should. In shining you provide a light for others, because even in the deepest and darkest darkness, when a light shines all eyes turn to it.

THE TRUST JUMP

Since she was about four years old, our youngest child, Dominique, has often called me into the hall, climbed five or six stairs, and then jumped into my arms. She has never asked me, 'Will you catch me Daddy?' She just jumps.

I love those kinds of moments, don't you? Dominique's jump causes me to feel 'trust' as my outgoing emotion. She leaps and trusts that I will always be there for her. I'm there for her because I know that she trusts me, I trust the fact that she trusts me, and I act accordingly. In doing so I become that trust.

I reproduce that trust as a Standard emotion when dealing with others. This is especially key when I am taking on new financial services or coaching clients. Regardless of what the new client is thinking, one of the Standards I hold for our connection is one of trust. This causes us both, via that connection, to act differently. All of us put trust in the wrong people at times. In my business life I recruited two people who proved that my trust had been misplaced. However, my experience is that a person's lack of integrity eventually proves a bigger problem for them than the problem they cause in the short term. I'm more learned now, but their way of being didn't change my core self, and in my TrueSelf I stay trusting future relationships.

When I speak at a financial-planning or self-help seminar I believe the audience senses my centeredness. They don't know how they feel trust, but they do. This is right for them and for me. They feel they want to be part of that 'something.' Among my clients are disproportionate numbers of accountants, former accountants, financial directors, and former financial directors. I have never targeted this sector. It's as if they notice that 'something' and they, for once, don't feel a need to left-brain or consciously figure 'it' all out before coming to a decision. When I'm with clients – whether corporate, personal coaching, or financial planning – I'm open and honest. I am true to myself because I know that the more I am, the stronger the connection.

GETTING SOME ANSWERS

When I finally woke up and listened to my TrueSelf, I was able to ask, and begin to answer, some of the big questions, such as 'Who am I?' and 'What is right for me?' When I look introspectively, feelings, thoughts, words, and guidance are there. Your TrueSelf has a voice and you need to listen. It may be expressed as feelings or thoughts, but know that it is the authentic 'You,' beneath the layers. Your TrueSelf will only guide you to do good things for yourself and others, never the contrary. The TrueSelf in all of us is steeped in love and, because we're all part of one thing, it will never seek to harm other human beings, who are after all another expression of it.

I recall the evening when I was exposed by the security guard's innocent question. In that naked place, where no other clothes would fit, I stood there and asked, 'Who am I? What is right for me?' I went deep inside myself, to my heart, my intuition, and what that TrueSelf shared with me was who I really was as a person, and this clothed me.

0–10 YOUR MOMENTS

Truth is 'me' and my TrueSelf is what I do now. Who are 'You'? What is right for you? Pause for a moment and think about why you are reading this book now. Maybe you've heard your true inner voice calling you too. Your TrueSelf is more powerful than your physical and thinking self combined. What is your TrueSelf saying to you now?

Happiness is in becoming what you can become.

CHAPTER **4**

Journey: To and from TrueSelf

From the moment I ran into the house from school that day I knew something was wrong. The house was full of relatives and yet so quiet, so I just stood looking through the window waiting for Mum's bus. I heard the low rumble and my heart leapt, but she didn't appear. Then I spotted my mother's friend Joyce running up the road, her long blue coat flapping. She arrived at the house and rushed in, crying and shouting, 'Mavis is dead.'

'Mavis is dead!' she said again.

Silently I stood there, dumbstruck. I knew only one thing: I didn't believe it.

The first woman that I ever loved had died, aged 36. Mavis was her pet name. Her real name was Kathleen Corilda Mills. Mum had gone into hospital for a routine operation, but afterward, in the hospital bed, had suffered a massive pulmonary embolism and died.

So what's the Journey I've been on? Looking back – and as Apple's Steve Jobs said, 'joining up the dots' – I saw the significance of my Journey and the whole unconscious philosophy it had produced. I made that philosophy conscious and accessed my Faculty and more, and I'm sharing that with you. By looking back, I trust that it will help you to join your dots and find the shape of things. And although I've now found my voice and calling, my Journey actually started when I lost my voice. And that was when my mother died when I was 13.

⏱ **Act now, for even a long life**
will seem short.

THE SECOND CHARACTERISTIC OF TRUESELF IS 'JOURNEY'

My parents were immigrants from Jamaica who came to the UK in the late 1950s and settled in Birmingham. They had come with their parents. My grandparents' journey is as much a part of the opportunity I face, and has been since my life began. They had run a good race and passed on the baton to the next generation – each leg of the journey a significant steer in the future legacy of the family and its members. I recall my sister Maxine saying, 'I remember those ancestors that I never met, but who are a part of me. I often think of their Journey too.'

I am the fifth of seven children, and growing up we were poor because my father worked in smelting, welding, and drop-forge factories most of his life, while my mother worked as an assistant in a hospital. When Mum died, Dad gave up his job in order to be mother and father to us children aged 7 to 17. He gave up a lot in doing this. Like all parents, he wasn't perfect; it was hard to be in such circumstances. Once more, I would like to thank him for doing what he did, and for getting us all through.

My mother's death affected me so deeply that for a few days after she died I couldn't speak, and when I did speak I had a profound stutter. No one spoke of it at home. On my first day back to school after the funeral I was asked to take my turn reading. I became tense and frightened. Little came out of my mouth but the strains of unformed sounds. I eventually managed to blurt out, 'C… C… C… Can't speak!'

Even with my eyes focused on the book, I could feel my classmates turning and looking at me, wondering what was wrong. I buried my head in my arms. I could hear the laughter and the murmurings of the other kids. Behind my closed eyes I had an image of those chuckling, curious faces.

My stammer followed me all the way though school and college, where I was nicknamed the 'stuttering parrot,' and into my early 20s. After I left college I did various menial jobs before I joined the financial services industry as a trainee broker and was taught to retail low premium savings and insurance schemes.

Your path often calls you home, yet you are too busy to notice.

A few years later, aged 24, I went on a mission to find out what was wrong with my speech and correct it. As I suspected, after medical investigation, there was nothing physically wrong; it was caused by the deep grief and trauma of losing my mother and the devastating realization when I was 13 that she wasn't coming back. On the day she died I knelt by my bed and prayed it was a mistake and that she would be back soon. I crawled under the bed as far as I could and cried. I lay there, desperately willing myself to sleep because I knew that when I woke up, this terrible nightmare would have vanished and Mum would be there again. That night I did, in fact, dream that it was all a big misunderstanding at the hospital, and we all were in the living room, and Mum was on the couch in her usual light blue dressing robe. Yet, when I woke the next day, I knew her death was real. Each of my siblings would have the same words to say of our mother: 'I really did love her and felt (in my heart) that she was the closest person to me in the world. She was just so easy to love,' for she meant the same to us all.

I couldn't bring her back when I was 13 and I couldn't bring her back when I was 24, but I was determined to find my voice again, and later I did.

⏱ *In life, without exception, every 'disadvantage' can eventually show itself as an 'advantage,' if you open up and let it.*

SELF-MADE TRAPS

Throughout our lives we see glimpses of our TrueSelf, but perhaps don't fully recognize or trust the path it shows us. And as a consequence of living as my NonSelf, poor business levels, and a speech impediment, my 20s and 30s were far from 'roaring.' I got myself into debt because, lacking in self-esteem, I overcompensated by spending money I didn't have, and built up substantial debts. I borrowed money just to live, and you know if you earn $1 and spend $1.05, you're in trouble.

My ever-increasing costs included fuel – traveling to visit my clients meant the miles really stacked up – reinvesting in the business, all the usual household bills, and bringing up a young family. It's no existence, just working and living to pay the bills. I remember trying to hide and disguise my threadbare suits, downtrodden shoes, and worn-out collars and cuffs from prospective clients. I also recall watching colleagues who enjoyed regular expensive vacations. Most years we had either no vacation or a cheap vacation, and they were harder to enjoy because I knew I'd have to work even longer hours to pay off the cost.

Looking back, it's no surprise that I was focused for so long on just earning money and the goal of having money, while ignoring for way too long the fact that inside I wasn't even living life as me – I was immersed in living as my NonSelf. I had created my own trap. I felt this acutely, but the lure of having 'money one day' kept me out of my TrueSelf. I had created my own island of illusion and was trapped as surely as a man behind bars, both of us culpable for our confinement.

The characteristics of Journey

LOSING TIME

A large part of my unhappiness stemmed from the fact that I spent so much time away from my family. Knowing the children were home having dinner killed me. Wherever I was I just wanted to be elsewhere – I was never present. I have since learned that wherever I am, I am there. Back then, when I was in the office or on the road, I longed to be at home for and with Gerry and the children. When I was at home, all I could think about was work and how to bring in the income. I was lonely, but it's 'not the kind of thing' that you can admit. I'm wiser now, and realize that loneliness is a state of mind that can be felt even in a busy life or room. Just like stress, loneliness is almost a taboo subject, but it shouldn't be. I know now that none of us are ever really alone, because we are all one, but we have to open up, keep reaching out to others, and find the connections.

At that time I really was trying – straining every mental and emotional sinew to become a success – but it seemed the harder I tried the tougher things became, and the more happiness and wealth eluded me. I wouldn't claim to have been an irresistible force, far from it, but I was under the illusion that I was meeting some immovable objects. I had plenty of reasons to set the world alight. I had goals, just like the experts had told me to, yet here I was, less than Mr. Average. I had a big enough 'why,' but I couldn't figure out the 'how.' This is part of the tragedy of not being your TrueSelf. As NonSelf you live under a cloud.

Most days I would leave home around 7 a.m. and not get back again until after 10 p.m. I even went into the office on Saturdays. The vast majority of this time was unproductive, but I felt it was the only honorable thing to do: to be there, doing some 'work.' Actually it just made me less resourceful, exhausted, and sad. Gerry wasn't happy with our lifestyle (she never said this, but I knew), but she accepted it and supported me, no matter what. Thank goodness, in spite of my huge imperfections, I'd married an angel.

As for the time with my children: I can't get it back. This is especially true of anyone working long hours chasing the 'mighty dollar.' This is an old way of thinking; it's somebody else's plan, not yours. You think that it will be okay later, that you'll have time with your children and wife/husband then, when you've got a bit more money in the bank. Don't you? This is flawed thinking. Apart from the fact that your future isn't guaranteed, you and your children will be different human beings in five or 10 years' time.

You know your date of birth, but you don't know your date of death, when this stage of your Journey ends. So why do we act as if extra life is a guarantee? Whatever you are, be it now. Whatever you want to do, in goodness and love, do it now. If you have children or parents to love and hug, do it now. Do you know that you have a tomorrow? Many is the man, and increasingly more women, who followed the old plan, only to find that when they were ready to be father/husband, or mother/wife their families were no longer ready to play the role expected of them. The world-renowned motivational speaker John Crudele said, 'Kids spell love T-I-M-E.'

🕐 *Love is a verb.*

LIVE ON PURPOSE

It's funny (or perhaps not) what stress does to you. In the last few years my wife and children recall and speak of things we've done and places we've been, but many times I don't know what they're talking about. This is because, when I was with them, all I could really think about was the bills. My mind was always someplace else. Even when I was there physically I wasn't there mentally, so I wasn't taking it in. This saddens me to this day. We pay a heavy price when we're not ourselves. Today, whenever I'm with my loved ones, I soak up the moments, I drink in the feelings, I mentally photograph the pictures, I store, I experience, and I remember.

I'm now aware of what was going wrong in my life: I was constantly focused on the future rather than my life right now – the present moment. With no anchor to the 'now,' we flounder. This isn't to say, 'live only for today,' rather that if we get the best out of ourselves each day, then all our tomorrows will be the best they can be for us. I know now that making money was my goal and my only focus in that period of my life. I could use the excuse that I had debts and bills to pay, but that's all it would be: an excuse. I know better now, don't you? Back then I didn't think about the higher Standards by which I could live my life each day, I only thought about my goal of getting money and then getting some more money.

For our world to be better we have to be happy from the inside out. We have an inner sagacity yearning to come out and lead us on the path that's right for us. Focusing on goals, you lose sight of what's important; what's in your present. For me, this meant that I lost sight of my family and who I was as a person. The more I followed this insane process the further I got from my family. The further I got from my family, the harder it became to make money and be happy. In this way, I was caught in a loop that just brought me more pain. Generally, we learn this lesson between the ages of 30 and 50, if we learn it at all. If we 'get it' much earlier we are twice blessed. It took me a long time and much pain to be on the wrong path. I was long on pain, but the solution was short.

I know that during my time in NonSelf I wasn't the greatest husband, father, brother, son, or friend. To my wife (my spiritual partner), my children, my family, and my friends (all of those who have blessed my life) to whom, because of my doubts and frustrations, failings, and faults I caused suffering, hurt, or anguish, or projected my inadequacy, I am truly sorry.

⏱ *Let your children know that, no matter what, you will never let go of their hand.*

LIVING FOR YOURSELF

Hueina Su lived much of her life under the cloud of her parents' disappointment. Her father had wanted a boy and let her know this almost daily, while her mother told her frequently, 'Hueina, you are not pretty and we are not rich, so you had better study hard.' Hueina became an overachiever and remained unhappy. When she moved to the USA from Asia in her 20s her fortunes didn't change: Men cheated on her and she became depressed and suicidal. One morning, a few years later, she woke up and realized that she'd just had enough of the old way of life: 'I mean I really woke up!' she says. She decided to live her life as the person she really was and to love herself. She intuitively knew that success would only come from this place: 'That moment saved my life.' She is now an international speaker and best-selling author on inner peace and confidence. She is open about the fact that she learned to understand and be grateful for her parents, and dedicates her books and career to them.

> ⏱ *You have responsibility because you have the ability to respond.*

Have you ever found it hard to change something in your life even though you knew it wasn't serving you, or may even be harming you? Sometimes we can become addicted to our pain and suffering. So how do we break ourselves from our addiction to stress, fear, low self-esteem, anger, poor habits, or abusive relationships?

I have met many people in my life who might argue that they have a right to be angry about their past, or their current situation, which was caused by events beyond their control. Tanya, abused by her mother and told she was unwanted; Keith, sexually abused as a child; Terrie, her home and assets stolen by her brother; Wendy, forced into early retirement by jealous, unscrupulous, and malicious superiors. And I've spoken with many others who lost their jobs due to company mismanagement, and others who have felt deep pain at losing loved ones.

All of these people have heartfelt stories. Yet it's an honor to the human spirit because, having undergone and escaped the toughest of times, carrying the effects and scars of the past, these people use their scars as a reason to continue to be good people – to love and to help others. To listen and be there for other people in their community, rich or poor.

What I learned from these people and my Journey is that you can use your past or present ordeals to prosper in some other way. Some people were able to literally let go or reframe past events by giving them a completely different meaning, and so carry on with a lighter load. Some were able to use past problems to positively change their lives. Whatever happened to you last week, or last year, or last decade, it may as well have happened to you in another life for all you can do about it. There is no past that you can re-inherit.

⏱ Thoughts are affected by other thoughts.

The loss of my mother, my stammer, near depression, and financial struggles are all things that I have reframed to shape me to become an agent of change for others and myself. I was, and still am, able to shift the direction of my energy from lack and unhappiness to self-discovery, joy, and contribution. The more I focus on these positive things from the inside out, the more I experience them because energy flows where attention goes. Now I'm my

TrueSelf at all times, with all people and in all things. Your TrueSelf is down to you. When would be a good time to start tapping into the abundance of your TrueSelf?

We get what's behind and through the door we continually open. In my heart I knew when I opened myself to my TrueSelf that all my grief, frustration, and stress would mean something positive in the future. I didn't know how, but I knew that I would eventually find a way to make it so. And I did.

⏱ *Why you are on this particular road?*

0–10 YOUR MOMENTS
· ·

The first part of living as TrueSelf is to say 'enough' to the old way of life. Perhaps it's time to open the suitcase and look honestly at what's inside, and then begin to remove the bars. Refuse to live in the past, and take ownership of your life today, just today, and do this each and every day, one day at a time. You can no more change your past than I can, but you can change how you represent its meaning to yourself and others, and therefore how you feel about it. In the meantime focus on the 'brand new present,' which is today, where you are always just you.

LIVE YOUR REAL LIFE FROM TODAY

I once heard one of the most successful life assurance agents in the USA say, 'I succeed because my purpose is stronger than my pain.' He meant it. He knows who he is, but he's better known for his charitable works and contributions to the community than for his financial services business. And I hope this anecdote makes it clear that your Journey to and of your TrueSelf doesn't have to start from a place of despair or wretchedness; it can start any time and any place that you're in right now.

There are many things that make an individual happy. It's different for us all, but you know it when you have it. It's a Journey of, to, and through your TrueSelf. You know where you're going and why, even if you don't yet know the 'how.' The path behind you takes on meaning and teaches you. I believe that everything in life happens for a reason, although the reasons are rarely given at that moment. In time they will be. Your focus is to become more aware of and stay on the path you were meant to navigate. Your TrueSelf plays your real rhythm, your music.

0–10 YOUR MOMENTS

This exercise will give you access to your TrueSelf. The more you listen to your TrueSelf, the stronger the connection you'll receive.

The first time you do this exercise, start by turning off your phone and putting away anything that might distract you.

Stop. Stand or sit in whatever way feels comfortable. When you're still, notice where your attention is...

If your attention is in your head, then bring your attention down to your heart, then to your solar plexus.

Now bring it down to your gut. Pause now, holding your attention there. Continue as you breathe from your stomach – allowing your diaphragm to expand and contract as you breathe in and out.

Center yourself by focusing on your breath.

Your attention is drawn inward when your eyes are closed, so close them when it feels the best thing to do. If you prefer, keep your eyes open and focus on a spot ahead of you. When you have found your focus, relax your eyes, and imagine that you can see past 180 degrees. Now imagine that you can see all around you, 360 degrees, as you relax your eyes into peripheral vision.

Keep your breath slow and low. In fact, you might find it helpful to place your hand on your stomach, covering your navel, and feel yourself breathing deeply and slowly.

As you do this you'll sense a shift from external consciousness to internal consciousness. You'll be focused on the present because you're focused on your breath – which is always in the now. When you are just being, in this place is your TrueSelf.

Now in this place relax...

Ask your gut a question, or give yourself an idea or thought. Imagine it's a game if you prefer. Ask yourself anything that was on your mind before you shifted to this place.

Whatever comes in response, allow it. Feel the shift as it goes back up through your solar plexus, your heart, and up to your head. You may even feel a sensation in your head as the response comes through. As long as the feeling comes from this place and your gut it will be your true feeling. Follow whatever guidance, instructions, or ideas come from that place.

With practice you'll be able to access your inner self or Truth in seconds, and then just by thinking about it – then you will have TrueSelf access. When it feels right you'll be able to access this place with your eyes open and in conversation, presenting, watching, reading, or studying. When you do, you'll begin noticing what you notice, and this will cause you to pay more relaxed attention to your TrueSelf and trust whatever positive messages come from that place – whether it's knowledge, an impulse, or an idea. In doing this you'll be following what the greatest minds have done. They used this approach to follow their passion and the plans that came from that centered place within.

Over time you'll be practiced in doing this and experience your Truth from there. You can also use this exercise whenever you're feeling pushed or pulled externally, awkward, or unsettled, to help you regain your inner calm, center, and balance. Your true power comes from within, without it you only have *little muscles* to power your achievements.

The choices we make in our 'moments' decide the next steps along the path for us. Think about your past life and how certain moments have brought you here. Every turn creates a new potential outcome. This is why Einstein said, 'You create your own universe as you go along.' It wasn't a metaphor, because we do, and he knew it!

🕐 *Bring the best of you to the surface.*
Most people don't and anyone can.

JOINING UP THE DOTS

In 2010 I attended the annual conference of the Professional Speaking Association (PSA) in the UK. I arrived early and found myself in a room of senior members of the association discussing another conference, the Global Speakers Summit (GSS), run by the Global Speakers Federation. The next GSS was taking place in Holland the following spring, when the best speakers from around the world would attend. The moment I heard this, I was certain I would speak there. Bearing in mind that my professional speaking career had started only months earlier you might consider this strange. Nevertheless, I took immediate action and booked as a delegate.

🕐 *Look for opportunities in every climate.*

Over the next few months I contacted the organizers and received a negative response because the speakers were already booked, but I wasn't deterred. And in February 2011 I instinctively felt I should send another e-mail to the GSS organizer. After pressing send, I was somewhat surprised to receive a reply minutes later. The respondent informed me that a speaker had just dropped out, and within an hour of my original e-mail, I received confirmation of having a slot at the GSS. Brilliant! I was able to speak and share my stuff.

The only way I can describe my speech at the GSS is to say that I experienced my time onstage as an extended moment in which I seemed to be above and disassociated from my self. Immediately afterward the feedback was positively incredible! People came up to me over the next couple of days saying so, including people who hadn't attended the session, but had heard of it and wanted to congratulate me. More than one delegate stated that my 'showcase' was the 'buzz' of the conference.

Moments of inspiration and intuition don't come to anything unless you're proactive about the nature of the message. Success is not a passive Journey; it's about taking action based on what comes to you from that centered place. Intuitive feelings from your TrueSelf without follow-up are useless. With follow-up they can lead to a 'shortcut' to your greatness.

In the conference hall that day were two people who would positively and deeply affect my Journey. The first was Maria Carlton, who was so taken with my content, story, and delivery she introduced me to the producer of a forthcoming self-help film with the USA's top success coaches, including Jack Canfield, Dr. John Gray, and Marci Shimoff. One week and one telephone call later I was in the movie as an expert.

The second was the owner of one of Europe biggest speakers' bureaus. They asked me to breakfast the next day and wanted to represent me in Europe. Even though my speaking career was in its infancy, they said I had 'something' and wanted to engage with that now. These were the guys who brought Bill Clinton to Europe after he left office, and who also represented Tony Robbins, one of the most successful personal-development gurus in the world. I just love how the universe works when you pay attention!

🕐 **Trust the connection.**

There are two Journeys: The Journey we take in life and the Journey to our TrueSelf. In reality the two Journeys are exquisitely entwined. To the degree you take one, you affect the other.

0–10 YOUR MOMENTS
. . . .

As you become the real 'You,' or whenever you need it, use the following mantra daily to help you on your Journey toward your TrueSelf:

I live my life as my TrueSelf each and every day. When I am in my TrueSelf, happiness comes to me and all those around me. I am aware of each and every

moment of my life and fully present with everyone
I come into contact with. I listen to my inner genius
and use its intuition to guide me. Today I will seek
out and create 10-second moments in my life.
I am my TrueSelf and I feel it serving me well.

My Journey toward my TrueSelf continues, and now I'm
holding a 'space' for you because I know that each of us
is on the very edge of an enormous breakthrough. Make
for yourself a larger life. Hold that place for yourself.
Keep focused on that true greater version of your life,
of you, and I promise that soon your life will begin to
change. Hold that space.

0–10 YOUR MOMENTS
· ·

When I think back to my Journey in NonSelf, it
felt like I was boxed in or carrying around a heavy
suitcase. Pause for a moment. Does this resonate
with you? What are you carrying that is slowing your
Journey? Carry it no longer on your road to freedom.
Where in your life might you have created a prison
for yourself? Begin to speculate about your Journey.
Pause. Where might you have taken a wrong turn,
an unintended detour? In which part of your life
might you be on the wrong path? TrueSelf is its
own Journey.

🕐 *Begin to find you.*

CHAPTER 5

Faculty: All these Gifts You Give to You

All I had to do was stand in front of a group of 15 potential recruits, introduce the Broker Principal, and then motion through a glass door for him to enter and give his talk. There I stood in front of what seemed like a sea of eager faces that slowly turned to bemusement as I stammered, stuttered, gasped, and spluttered whenever I tried to say a few simple words. Sweat ran down my face and my wet shirt stuck to my back. Somehow I finally managed to blurt out, 'I g... g... give you D... D... Dennis G... Green.' It was possibly one of the worst moments of my life. I'm not sure whether Dennis ever found out how badly that introduction went, but a month later I received a letter from one of the potential recruits expressing her disappointment at not being taken on by the firm. She ended her letter with '...how I was not taken on, when someone like you Mr. Mills can be working for the company. Someone who can't even speak properly and babbled incoherently...'

Until the day that letter arrived I had been living an illusion. I accepted my speech impediment as being part of 'me.' I managed my business on a one-to-one basis, by telling myself my stammer caused clients to draw close to me and listen. But the day that letter arrived I decided it had gone on long enough. Regardless of her intention, the author of that letter was right about my speech. I made a decision to learn to speak properly for the second time in my life. I sat back and told myself, 'Everybody can speak… and what's more, I will wake up and find myself one of the finest speakers of my generation.' I didn't go on a course for stutterers because I didn't want to be a stutterer. I went on a Dale Carnegie course for public speaking because I wanted to learn to speak.

It was a pivotal time in my life, as I realized I had a gift for speaking. Later, when I found my TrueSelf, I fully realized my talent and began to shine. Often when I speak now my breath works through me, and I feel as if my whole being is in the room. When I'm in this place my clients and audiences feel it too, and they have told me, at some level, it reminds them of their own path and that they want to be airborne, too.

🕐 *Uncover your pot of gold.*

THE THIRD CHARACTERISTIC OF TRUESELF IS 'FACULTY'

Faculty is our hidden talents, abilities, and skills. We don't regularly tap into it, but when we do, we awaken the genius within. You may have first accessed and used your gifts and talents when you were a child, or early on in your adult life. You may have thought of your Faculty as a 'state' you were in, or described it as 'I don't know what was happening, I don't know how I did that.' You may even have laughed it off when challenged about how and why you performed so incredibly well, unlike your normal self. You dismissed your Faculty because you were too busy in your life to notice what was really happening in and around you.

🕐 *Those that use their Faculty move to their top quickly and stay there longer.*

When you're living and working without your greatest abilities at play, life is no joke. You may have noticed that you're on a treadmill, without the time or inclination to look left, right, or up. At times you might feel as if you're running just because the treadmill is moving faster. Occasionally, however, you may have caught yourself in the right space inside yourself, with everything working out exceptionally well, and you perform at an exquisite level. You perhaps called it being 'in the zone' or 'in the flow.' But when the moment passed you got on with ordinary life. You might not have realized the significance of what had just taken place, but these moments are actually when you're in your Faculty. It's rather like discovering you have a superpower, only to ignore it because you're too busy getting on with your life. If you found you could fly, you wouldn't ignore it would you?

If you stay in NonSelf you'll be trapped in a world that you didn't choose and not of your liking. Until now, what in your life was so important that it stopped you bringing your very best into each day? I know from personal experience that empty promises (goals) prevented me from living presently and experiencing my Faculty. One way you'll know whether this is true for you too, is if you're living in your head constantly. Are you always overthinking things? If so, then you're pulling away from the seat of your power – your instinct and intuition. To go back to your Faculty, you have to come down out of your head and into what you feel. The main traps of NonSelf are:

- Staying in a job you dislike for the lure of a pay rise.

- Accepting the judgments of others – either remembered from your past or in your present – about who or what you are and what you can achieve. Only you know the Truth.

- Allowing other people's limiting beliefs to affect your thinking.

- Doing what you're told, rather than thinking for yourself.

- Listening to friends or relatives who tell you what you need to do to be happy, when they are disillusioned and unhappy themselves

- Sheepishly following the industry norms and not thinking about whether those norms are right for you.

- Striving to reach goals and targets set outside of you, particularly if set by your employer or partner without your consultation and input.

Certain events and moments take us into our TrueSelf, and it's usually when we're experiencing a heightened level of excellence – whether in sports, sales, business, or learning – which we might describe as being in the flow or the zone. These moments might seem accidental, as if we're not able to control them, yet they allow us to access knowledge and proficiency for long enough to hold the moment and be present. In these moments we're no longer in NonSelf; we've escaped the shackles that bind us to ordinary performance and experience, to something more extraordinary.

There is a power within you, and when you bypass the conscious mind and work from intuition and instinct anything can happen. When you use your Faculty, life will be noticeably easier for you.

🕐 *Show your masterpiece.*

'MUSIC MAESTRO, PLEASE'

Like many children, Albert Frantz was given piano lessons when he was eight. To the dismay of his parents, his third piano teacher brought him home, refunded his tuition fees, and said that he would never play the piano. You would have thought this was the end of Albert's musical career, but, years later, a moment at college caused Albert to stop. As he wandered past the music faculty he heard Gershwin's *Rhapsody in Blue*. The music resonated with something inside him, and he knew he had to play it on the piano. So Albert went away alone to learn it, and found that he could play it, without the decade of training normally required. Years later, when we met for lunch in London, Albert described the moment that he played the piece by ear: 'It was like discovering that I had a superpower, I could just play the piece.' Albert went on to huge success and won a Fulbright Scholarship to study in Vienna, where he now lives, teaches, and is a concert pianist having accessed and realized his Faculty. What is within will astound you, if you let it.

USING YOUR INTUITION

When top business people, elite sports stars, and super-salespeople speak of Faculty they refer to it in the same way that you would. I would like to say that it doesn't matter what we call it, but it does. Our linguistic interpretation transforms the 'meaning' of everything. But you don't have to be an elite athlete to know about the 'zone' and 'flow,' because they're known across the globe and in all cultures. Although it has different names, it refers to a powerful energy that exists and is known around the world even though it is invisible.

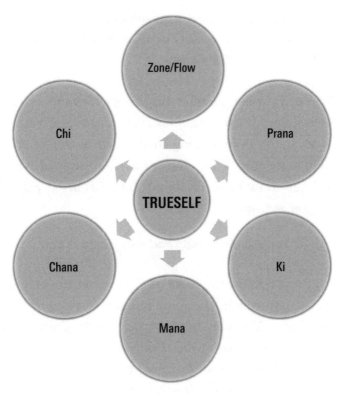

The characteristics of the Faculty of TrueSelf

0–10 YOUR MOMENTS

Think of a time when you were in the zone or flow; a time when you performed so outstandingly at a meeting, in a sales presentation, on the sports field, or in a relationship, you marked that time as being exceptionally different to normal. You might have known something you didn't actually know, or had an overwhelming urge to do something different, with magical or brilliant results. Take your time now

to remember those moments and write them down.
Remember them in every detail, as they'll help you
know your TrueSelf Faculty.

Whether your last moment was when you were a child,
10 years ago, or last year, your Faculty is as much a part
of you as the heart beating in your chest. All of your
Faculties are just 'You,' and are at your disposal when
you know how to access them. Your Faculty is part of
who you are, not a thing you do.

⏱ *You are everything and everything is you.*

How do you know this to be true? Well, when you're in
the zone you couldn't do those things unless you *could do*
those things. You couldn't have performed at a brilliant
genius level unless you were a brilliant genius performing.
What you called the zone or flow was a glimpse of what
you are, the real 'You.' It was your TrueSelf shining, if
only for a moment. Simply put, your Faculty is 'You.'
You didn't go into any zone or enter any flow state, you
just accessed more of the real you or, in some cases, a lot
more of you. Whatever you did is only because *you could*.

Some people may not have felt this characteristic of
TrueSelf the way it is described here, or not experienced
what others – incorrectly – call a zone or flow state.
Meditating on your TrueSelf gifts will increase your
abilities and power of focus. When I say meditate, I don't
mean sitting cross-legged up a mountain somewhere. In
just the briefest of moments you can learn a way to access
your Faculty. You can do this now if you like.

0–10 YOUR MOMENTS
· ·

Take a deep breath, notice your breath, and pay attention to where you are breathing in your body. As you focus on your inward breath, plant your feet flat on the floor. Let your body relax and notice how it just supports itself. Make use of your peripheral vision, keeping full awareness of the room. Every detail is available to you. Breathe out.

Take another deep, slow breath – expanding your stomach and lower diaphragm, not your chest – focus on your breath and then bring your attention inside to the center of your breath. If you wish, now you can close your eyes, because this enables you to cut off any external stimulation.

Now continue your slow, deep breathing from this centered place and think about you. As you do, smile inwardly. Stay still and relaxed. In this state of relaxed consciousness you're in the best place for planting seeds of change. Bring to mind your best abilities and the people you love deeply. Consider your gifts, your talents, and abilities now.

Ask yourself if you're willing to make great leaps in your personal energy and power, right now. Listen to the answer.

Now think back to a time when you performed at a level that surprised you with its clarity, power, and energy. Remember what you were doing, and what was happening inside of you. Bring back those feelings – they are all inside of you – and recognize the difference between that feeling and how you usually feel.

You chose this moment because you know that you were different in it, something in you had shifted. Notice how – as you stay in that place where you had greater knowledge, abilities, confidence, or awareness – you activate more of those feelings in you now. Continue to re-create that feeling in you now. Now, for as long as you like, or as long as you can, hold that space.

With practice this mini-meditation will take you back to this place of awakening within moments, so you'll have a way of reminding yourself and glimpsing your Faculty. The more you trust that your Faculty exists and is real, the more it will guide you as it trusts you to listen and allow it space. Behave as if that were true until it is for you. Until you do this, you'll have no idea of the extent of your Faculty. What I have found is that you can tune in and direct your Faculty to a particular task or issue and find a power available like no other that you met in your NonSelf hours.

THE SPORT OF KINGS

Before I even hit the ball I knew it was going to be a perfect shot, even though I had no right to make it. There I was, galloping on my pony Gato, some 150 yards from the goal. I felt the whole world in my awareness, the sound, the breathing of Gato and the other players, and the pitch. I was deep in my Faculty. I hit the ball with my stick and the ball flew high up into the air, over half the length of the field and through the goal. I repeated a shorter pass later in the game, sending the ball over the opposition players' heads, to my teammate Michael Hall, who went on to score. Later, I overheard Jason Dixon, the former England polo captain, say to another coach, ' I taught him that,' to which the other coach, Glen, replied, 'No, I taught him that.' They chuckled, and so did I as neither man taught me. What I did in that moment they didn't teach me! I just got myself into my TrueSelf and accessed Faculty, having seen and learned the basics of polo, and without being able to ride a horse just four years earlier. Now I could ride and was performing shots and passes that many higher handicap members of the polo fraternity struggled to do with consistency. It's easier to access latent gifts and talents when you are in TrueSelf.

Earlier in my polo-playing career I had done similar things. I once played and scored tactically so well that it caused Claire Tomlinson, the highest-ever-handicap female English polo player, England coach, and friend of HRH Prince Charles, to say loudly to me, 'YOU'VE GOT IT, you're a polo player! YOU'VE GOT IT.' Back then I wasn't sure what 'IT' was, but I was pleased with what IT was producing for me. Back then I couldn't ride a horse – some say I can't ride properly now, and that's probably true – but I had found the benefit of tapping into my Faculty at will.

I enjoyed my time playing polo. Whatever the status and grandeur of a club I was always welcomed. At one particular social occasion, I was dancing with Gerry when she locked my gaze with her beautiful brown eyes, and with a subtle head gesture, urged me to look over my shoulder. When I did, I was amused to realize that I was dancing directly back-to-back with HRH Prince William. TrueSelf: You Rock! It's funny, or perhaps it isn't, when a 'nobody' from the inner city, child of immigrants, can find themselves. It's the fun of TrueSelf.

🕐 *Capture your thoughts and ideas and then they will serve you.*

Many words, thoughts, questions, phrases, or ideas can cause an immediate shift in us that didn't occur before. If you accept the Faculty characteristic of TrueSelf, then the following idea will change you: What if, instead of being in your TrueSelf Faculty once many years ago, you could be in your Faculty once a year? What success could you create if you were in your Faculty once a month? Once a week? Each and every day? What could your life be like if you were your inner genius many times through your day and over many months and years? Imagine how this could increase your personal success and happiness? Just imagine the results if the very best of you was in your world each day. Now what does your life look like?

0–10 YOUR MOMENTS

As you ponder the potential meaning of that idea and what it might mean for your life, think about the following questions, and write down your thoughts.

What are you doing in your life **not** to be in your TrueSelf Faculty?

What are you allowing to keep you from your inner genius?

While you might fear that you're only a genius in random moments, the truth is that you are a genius beyond measure. The TrueSelf Faculty is the normal state yet, in ignorance or by neglect, we allow the world to take us and keep us out of it. It's time to stop letting your friends, your family, your boss, the newspapers and TV, and the world at large tell you who and how to be.

I tuned into my inner genius and became a professional speaker, author, mentor, and successful financial services professional. Even when I think back to the letter from that young lady while in my 20s, it was my inner genius that gave me the idea not just to speak but also to be one of the finest speakers of my generation. Both the above shifts came from within, not without. The same Faculty led me to become an executive producer of the award-winning movie *Of Mary*, and then to speak in such a unique way that I was chosen to co-star in my first international personal development movie. It led me to know which route to go in order to share platforms with some of the world's greatest teachers and success coaches. In the last few years, I've spent so much time in my TrueSelf, using my Faculty, that my life has shifted into the stuff of dreams. God willing, I have plenty more road to travel.

If it's your intention to increase your happiness quotient as a result of using this philosophy, it should be obvious that you can do that now. If, however, you want to raise your sense of fulfillment and contentment, then the TrueSelf characteristic of Faculty will give you that, as it will enable you to tap into the inner genius which lives within all of us.

🕐 *Step beyond the area that*
you are operating in.

USING YOUR FACULTY

For many years I've spoken in front of audiences in order to share my philosophy for success or wealth management. Without fail, I stand there until I get a certain feeling. The feeling tells me that I'm in the right place internally to present magically. I feel it from my gut to the top of my head down to my feet planted on the floor. This is the place that I recognize as being deep in my TrueSelf, and it is like being back in my office for my 10-second moment after the security guard's question. When in this place, I'm able to connect with an audience at a level that is beyond a conscious connection. In that place I know that inside the individual members of the audience is something unconscious that is connected with me. When I'm in TrueSelf I can fully associate with exactly what I'm doing and saying, while at the same time remaining disassociated and actually noticing the dynamic between me and the group, as if I were a third party looking in.

Most of the time I use my peripheral vision. (When I'm not in my TrueSelf this feeling, the connection, the extra information, is not present.) While presenting, I'm fully alert and sharp, and practice being still inside. In all my years since learning of my TrueSelf I've never had a bad audience. I believe that this is because of the space that I hold and the connection that we have. Potential financial-service-seminar presenters have come to my seminars in the past for mentoring, and one of the questions they always ask is, 'What do you do when you get a bad audience, a heckler, a really negative person who throws you?' or something along those lines. My response is and will always be, 'I only ever have great audiences,' and it's true. I know that some of those same audience members might be problematic for another presenter, even if they gave the same presentation. Where you are internally allows others to be in a different state of mind and intention in relation to you.

VISION OF A WELSH WIZARD

Ryan Giggs was one of the greatest soccer players ever, and is still the most decorated player in the English Premier League and the world. Ryan gained fame because of his ability to run past the opposition and do incredible things with the ball. In his very late 30s he still played for Manchester United, one of the most successful soccer clubs in the world. While I'm not a fan of the club, I am a fan of the power and Faculty Ryan accessed during his career, which made him one of the greatest players in the history of the game. Ryan once shared how he got in the 'flow' when he played. He spoke about the way that he often gets into a place where his foveal (central) vision drops away and he sees instead with peripheral vision. He described how in that place, everything else around him seemed to slow down. I don't know about you, but I figure that if you can play any sport or engage in any physical activity with an expanded vision and your opponents seem to slow down, would it be any wonder that you could play like a wizard?

This ability to access your Faculty is not limited to sports or public speaking, of course. In ordinary life, in business, and in sales you can be in that place and be wizard-like when you connect with your core and from there to others. I have often been in meetings where I feel myself dissociating from the room, and can literally see and hear myself speaking from within, while at the same time being fully aware of what is going on in the room. From this place of double-association, words, thoughts, questions, phrases, and ideas have come to me that have perhaps helped me to take the meeting into a different direction, or to provide an intuitive insight into the business in hand. No one else has access to my Faculty. Mine is as unique to me as yours is to you.

It doesn't matter how intellectually clever someone is, when you are in TrueSelf, the right thing happens. While many people somehow get stuck in their brains – only accepting what they can weigh, count, and measure – by relaxing and centering my attention on my inner self, breathing from my lower diaphragm with my feet flat on the floor, with relaxed peripheral vision, I slip into TrueSelf mode. From here I'm able to listen and feel my way through the dialogue and potential issues: listening and feeling for the intuition that comes up. I have no college degree and I know that true wisdom comes from within.

I always let my financial- or personal-coaching clients know not to expect a big closing question at the end of discussions, because there won't be one. If we're in the right place, we do business. If the unconscious relationship or connection isn't right at that point, we don't. I never try to browbeat someone into doing business with me. If I'm doing that then I'm in the wrong space, and so are they. I simply trust my TrueSelf; I trust the process and I am often guided and inspired by the power of my Faculty. There is a Tao of closing without closing.

FACULTY WINDFALL

This is just one of the many bonuses to TrueSelf Faculty. I've worked as a coach and mentor for many years now and the people whom I mentor and guide are usually those considering stepping onto their path or who have already begun their Journey to TrueSelf, while others are curious about what is within them. I always ask them the following five questions. These are based upon their previous understanding of the TrueSelf, so my language is initially one of 'flow' or 'zone.'

> **DM:** 'When you were last in the zone/flow, how much fear did you feel?'
> **Client:** 'None.'
> **DM:** 'How much indecision did you feel when you were in that place?'
> **Client:** 'None.'
> **DM:** 'How much doubt did you feel there?'
> **Client:** 'None.'
> **DM:** 'How much embarrassment?'
> **Client:** 'None.'
> **DM:** 'How much rejection did you feel while in the zone or flow?'
> **Client:** 'None.'

Whenever I ask a question about the presence of negative emotions and negative influences of a person who is living in their TrueSelf, the answer always comes back a resounding 'none,' and it always will. When you're in your TrueSelf Faculty there isn't any negative limiting resource, only positive empowering resource. The answer always comes back as 'none' because you're connected to your greater self and Faculty, which can do for you far more than you may currently accept. For a moment now, consider the above questions for yourself.

You'll begin to realize you're in TrueSelf when you feel centered and have an absence of negative or destructive emotions and thoughts, because your TrueSelf doesn't know these things. You know you're living more of your Truth and what is meant for you when indecision, doubt, and irrational fear begin to loosen their hold and effect on you.

Negative emotions, like fear, are contagious. Like all emotions they radiate a signal. When you feel fear, it radiates out from you. Humans can catch fear; animals too. When I first learned to ride at Beaufort Polo Club, and later at Royal Leamington Spa, I was scared of horses, always had been, and the horses always played up for me and were agitated and unruly, even though they would behave perfectly for others and for the coaches. At the time I didn't believe that it was my energy transmitting to the 'dumb horse.' I know better now. When I was centered and relaxed, my polo ponies became orderly and gradually reacted to me as if they were part of me. I did this by literally breathing in and out positive feelings of 'OKness,' as if my breath came in and out of my body, originating from my gut. I imagined myself as part of the pony; getting into rapport with its rhythm and then being able to change it because I was able to ride as if we were one. In my mind's eye, I shifted my center of gravity to somewhere between the two of us. When I got it, I rode keeping myself in peripheral vision, not trying to *do* anything except imagining that I was just *being*, with a beautiful sense of calm at my core. From this place magic happened.

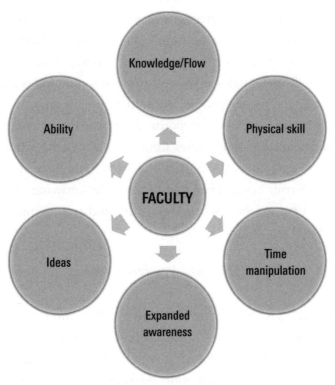

The characteristics of 'Faculty,' or being in 'flow'

When you're in TrueSelf you're linked to everything else around you. We're part of the universe so our genius and power come not just from within us but from outside too. One single entity is all that exists and we are each an expression of it. This one field – where each thing expresses itself in many ways – gives you access to all power and knowledge. Power, at its greatest level and intention, is love. The TrueSelf is the channel or Conduit connecting us all.

When we're off balance it's because we're not tuned in to our TrueSelf and all that it can access. Indecision, doubt, and fear are sure signs that you are too far from your TrueSelf state to be most effective. Your TrueSelf plays your real rhythm, your music. When you're in TrueSelf others will see the real powerful you, and react accordingly. Other people, without knowing why, will gravitate to you and act positively toward you. Your intuitive information comes from your TrueSelf, which informs your nervous system and body, which in turn informs your brain. Then you become the knowing. We know first and best when we are in, and pay attention to, TrueSelf.

🕐 Is this who you really are?

TrueSelf has never let me down. We don't make mistakes as TrueSelf, as it can't be wrong, it can just be more right, for us. To maximize your inner comfort and the outer worldly benefits of being in your TrueSelf, begin to harmonize your thoughts, think positive and healthy thoughts, and the power that serves you will be good power. Keep your connection at the right frequency and you'll strengthen that connection through use, in the same way a muscle gets stronger with exercise, but atrophies through lack of use.

THE INTUITIVE HEART

The late co-founder of Apple and Pixar, Steve Jobs, at his world-famous 2005 Stanford commencement address, advised that we should use 'our intuition.' Here he was at the height of his powers and achievement, with the world hanging onto his every word. He spoke not of his business acumen, not of his achievements, not of a business model or of logical business processes that would help the attentive future leaders in his audience. What he did say remains one of the most profound statements ever made by a man of such high commerce and stratospheric wealth. Steve Jobs simply spoke of his Journey in three easy-to-get stories, and then implored us to trust our hearts and our intuition. What did he know? What power had he tapped into that he relayed to us in his most simple, yet most profound address? Did you get it then? Do you get it now? I trust that you do. Somewhere there was a message.

BE FEARLESS

If you're in the habit of living in your head too much, beware. What keeps us out of our TrueSelf is staying too conscious, which means overanalyzing and thinking too much. The other thing that keeps us away from following our hearts and intuition is the fear of what other people may say. We worry about what the world will say if we step out with our 'own' clothes on, letting the world know that it is they who are really wearing the emperor's clothes. It's better to stand naked and honest than to clothe yourself in lies and deceit. As Leonardo da Vinci so eloquently said, 'Simplicity is sophistication.'

It is better to walk your Truth than to ride in a vehicle of pretense, because when you reach the end of your Journey, you'll know yourself for sure. It takes more courage to walk your path, but the rewards are infinite.

Being in NonSelf keeps us from our higher selves. In NonSelf we're more easily controlled and influenced by the outside world. We wait for the world's approval and its directions. But have you noticed that many people are rarely helpful and positive in assisting you? Most people are lost, but few will admit it, and yet they still tell others what to do. It isn't wise to trust the directions of those who are themselves lost. The world is full of lost people, and it is also inhabited by mainly negative people.

The more negativity that surrounds you, the more it occupies your mind, but it doesn't just stay there, it moves into your body. You might often have felt your heart flutter in angst, fear, or dread. These signals originate in your head and then transfer to your gut and make you feel fearful. This is important to note because if this is how you live inside then you'll transfer it to your outside world, too. But you can use that same process in reverse. From a centered, trusting, optimistic, positive perspective you can send the right messages to your heart and mind. When your inner genius is turned on, it will support you best with empowering, positive, self-affirming communication.

You experience your Faculty as hunches, ability, inspiration, and intuition because they are the language TrueSelf uses to communicate with you. When you experience TrueSelf you are experiencing your core. Whatever you think you are, you are always, in all ways, more than that.

🕐 *We 'know' first in our TrueSelf.*

BE GUIDED BY YOUR INNER GENIUS

At times I'm guided to go to a meeting, ask a question, or just be still, listen, and wait for the right time to act, speak, or respond. I've also been given insights and ideas that come from my TrueSelf and give me connection to everything else. At times like this, I'm guided to call a client, go see someone, to break rapport with someone who I feel doesn't have my best interests at heart, or I am suddenly given an idea that solves a problem. I'm not saying that I merely think this; I am stating that I am guided by my intuition to feel this, and those feelings give me a steer. As long as I hold my TrueSelf space I'm in my personal power – my Faculty. That intelligent energy guides me and comforts me, in love.

0–10 YOUR MOMENTS
••••••••••••••••••••••••••

Can you feel or see your Faculty yet? For the longest
time I couldn't see mine but now it flows and fills
me. Yours may still feel like the faintest glimmer,
but it's there in You. Give life to, and live as, your
inner genius.

*⏱ Everything that is in your life
originates within you.*

CHAPTER 6

Conduit: Intelligent Energy

At the end of 2007, the FTSE 100 closed at 6,457 points, and the turmoil in the world financial markets continued. In November 2008, one of the financial foundations I support ran a competition to raise money for good causes. For a donation of £20 we were invited to guess the closing price of the FTSE 100 at the end of the year. The prize was the index amount in cash. At first I made a few educated guesses, based upon the state of world affairs, the market and Elliott waves, but as I sat there I became centered and an idea came to me. It didn't need any calculation or a financial model. It was just a pure idea, along with an absolute sense of certainty that the FTSE 100 would be at 4,434 at the end of December. I sent in my entry form and let it go... until December 31, when I got a phone call telling me I'd won and the index had finished at 4,434. I think the caller from the foundation was surprised when I laughed at his news, but I knew I'd win because I knew my 'hunch' from my TrueSelf was right. I put the phone down and laughed again when I told my wife that we were now £4,434 richer.

Where did that information come from? What space was I in that allowed me to tap into a far greater source of knowledge than my Faculty contained? How much richer would the man or woman be who could access their TrueSelf, and then trust what came from that place? The answer to the second question depends on the intention of the man or woman. The answer to the first question is 'intelligent energy,' pure and simple.

There are many moments when my TrueSelf just gives me raw facts, data or information that I didn't learn in the traditional sense. Perhaps it is, as I believe, because we're all part of the same body – in other words we're all interconnected to each other and the universe. If this is true then it stands to reason that the information available to one part of the system is available or useful to another, if and when they are in harmony. Being in rapport with your TrueSelf creates inner harmony and you'll oftentimes find information given to you from that place.

⏱ *There is greater wealth inside you*
than in any bank.

THE FOURTH CHARACTERISTIC OF TRUESELF IS 'CONDUIT'

I'm not alone in believing that there exists an intelligent energy that binds everything together: The physical and nonphysical. From Socrates to Einstein, da Vinci to Curie, from Rumi to Hawkins, Michelangelo to Seacole, all have been able to touch something from outside themselves to 'create' new beauty. Their life stories tell how many of them literally tuned in to the universe for ideas. All our information originates from within us or from that universal storehouse.

Predicting the exact closing figure of the FTSE 100 didn't come from my intellectual or conscious self. It came through the Conduit – the pathway or connection to everything else that is – to my TrueSelf. There's no way this information was actually inside me as a resource to be dipped into. What came to me was from the same source that has inspired people throughout history. Hundreds of the world's greatest minds have attested to having been inspired by an idea from out of nowhere, 'from the ether.' They knew what they knew, and they knew what they didn't. Yet those men and women, some of whom we now call geniuses, were in their TrueSelf. In this place the 'unknown,' that 'something,' put in an appearance via Conduit.

Neither you nor I have to prove the existence of Conduit, we just have to do what the other geniuses did. Accept and use it with known principles. There is a storehouse of information and humans, with application, can literally pluck ideas and solutions from this intelligent energy. The inventor Thomas Edison described this energy as 'infinite': 'I know this world is ruled by infinite intelligence. Everything that surrounds us – everything that exists – proves that there are infinite laws behind it. There can be no denying this fact. It is mathematical in its precision.'

There is a Law of Connection which tells us that there are no spaces between things. Even where there is a vacuum, scientists now know the space is filled with another kind of matter. All types of matter are energy. There are no spaces, so everything is connected at the tiniest, so far unfathomable, level. The entire universe is filled with yet more energy and types of matter waiting to be discovered. As physicists search for the Higgs boson and other infinitesimally small particles of energy, I'm convinced that in 1,000 years we'll be searching for yet smaller particles and energy components: Searching the cosmos for what makes energy do what it does.

While the search is on for the 'God particle' I wonder what the scientists are doing with the particles we already know about. What are the ways to make use of what we know, but can't see? I know how to drive my car, but some other intelligent energy put it together and yet another designed the internal combustion engine. Me? I just drive it from A to B and enjoy the ride. As I touch my finger to the keyboard, I am as connected to it now as I am to the girl sitting on the corner of Belasis Road in Mumbai. Our energy is the same, because we are all connected energetically and spiritually. Hence the energy and intelligence is available to our 'connective' and can be utilized by 'the one.' The 'one' in this case is you. This is the Law of Connection.

🕐 *Everything is connected to everything.*

USING TRUESELF TO SOLVE UNSOLVABLE PROBLEMS

When the greats of ancient and modern times had done all they could mentally do and were stuck or baffled by whatever was occupying their time, they put themselves in 'the quiet place' and ruminated on their intentions until the desired information or ideas came from outside of them. As Thomas Edison advised, 'The best thinking has been done in solitude.'

When in our TrueSelf we're able to open a Conduit to knowledge or intelligent energy outside ourselves. Occupying that place tunes us like a radio in to that 'something' greater. Inspiration comes, too, from within your Faculty. All this happens when we're in our inner genius. Being in my inner genius allows me to connect at a deeper level with 'something' else, and it is this Conduit to that something else that shows me the awesome power of being in TrueSelf.

0–10 YOUR MOMENTS

Read the previous paragraph again and pause to consider its implications. Now pause again, just for a few seconds, as you notice what words, thoughts, questions, phrases, and ideas come up for you. Capture what comes from this place because it will serve you.

🕐 *Nurture your TrueSelf as you would a child.*

INNER GENIUS POWER

You can utilize this intelligent energy to know when to make a phone call, where to go, even where to sit. Or you can use it to enhance or save a life. In the past you might have had hunches and perhaps followed through on them, maybe not. In the past you might have had an urge to call a family member or friend, only to hear them say, 'Wow, I was just thinking about you this second.'

Have you ever been curious, I mean really curious, about what's happening in those instances? Why everyone has similar experiences of this? What is this connection that exists but doesn't have any cables – in fact, no physical or visual clues at all? The Law of Connection states that we're all connected 'wirelessly' though the ether. It's only through lack of belief, use, and application that we don't benefit more from the unified field that makes up our connective. Try it.

All things are connected. And because we are one thing, everything affects everything else. Therefore when we harm another living thing (and all things are living) we directly or indirectly harm ourselves. The Conduit to intelligent energy connects us to all people and information, even when it's formed in another person's mind, the air, the trees, the ground and the animals – including the lions, tigers, and bears. Conduit warns you about dangers outside.

🕐 *Trust the 'stuff.'*

WHY LOOK BACK?

Ben Saunders, the Polar explorer, is a friend and, at the time of writing, he is one of only three people to have skied solo to the North Pole, and the youngest to do so by some 10 years. *The Times* in the UK called him 'The next Ranulph Fiennes.' Ben describes an episode where he avoided death by following his intuition. Three days into a trek to the North Pole, all he could see out of his hood and goggles was snow and his skis. Every day he went forward, focused, never looking back – there was really no point in looking back. On the third day, with no auditory or visual clues, he had an inner compulsion to look over his left shoulder and saw a polar bear – top of the food chain in the North Pole! The polar bear was eventually put to flight by a warning shot from Ben's sawn-off shotgun (something polar explorers always carry, apparently, in case of run-ins with bears). When we met for lunch I only had one question for him: 'What made you stop and look back?' I must admit his response didn't surprise me: 'A feeling really, just a feeling.'

What was that 'feeling'? How was it able to guide him away from mortal danger? What else can that feeling do? Where does it come from? Can we, by design, access that feeling to guide us more, even against logic?

You may never cross the North Pole solo, but begin to imagine the power of your TrueSelf guiding you in your business and life, the same way it guided Ben Saunders. Conduit gave Ben the 'feeling,' because it couldn't come from any other place, and it saved his life. Ben was used to being alone and concentrating on his abilities to guide him, and if you continually work at strengthening any connection, just like widening a water supply pipe, it serves you better.

This is how Conduit works. As a result of being in your TrueSelf you literally go to a place where the connective sinew is strengthened. You appear like a genius, when in fact all you're doing is applying the Law of Connection, which we'll explore in more depth in Part II. In the meantime I'd like to share some more thoughts with you.

DEEPAK CHOPRA AND FRIENDS

In 2011 I purchased four tickets for An Audience with Deepak Chopra. I don't know why I purchased them, it just felt right. The same day a prospective financial-planning client told me, 'Deepak Chopra is the one teacher that I truly follow!' In my 25 years in the financial services industry this was a unique incident. 'Ha, so that's why I purchased the extra ticket,' I thought. I offered the ticket as a gift and the client accepted.

A few months later my Executive Assistant, Sonja Graham, was reviewing hotels in Carlsbad, California, for a meeting the following month. She's great, and always efficient in caring for the wealth of the business, so when I looked at her list and asked her to book the La Costa Resort and Spa, she queried why, because it cost more than the hotel she'd chosen. But I picked it because it 'felt' right. A month later, as I wandered around the grounds of the exceptionally beautiful La Costa, I was informed that I had inadvertently booked into the only hotel in the world containing The Chopra Center of Wellbeing.

I attended a yoga class and afterward met the only other people who remained in the room, Tanya Pergola, Dr. Bonnie Macdonald, and Dr. Mark McGinley. It was Tanya who asked if anyone would like to do a session in the mediation room. I had a strong sense of a pre-existing connection with the three, so it was the most natural thing when we all said 'Yes' simultaneously. After the session we shared dinner and a conversation about philosophy, and I learned they were all Certified Deepak instructors who had flown in to take part in the program that week. Mark, Bonnie, and Tanya are all centered and open, and it's a joy to be with them.

Meeting such wonderful people and helping each other on our Journeys is the most natural state of being. That is what we do for and with one another, and it's how things should be.

The American author Wallace Wattles wrote, 'There is a thinking stuff from which all things are made, and which, in its original state, permeates, penetrates, and fills the interspaces of the universe.' In other words, inspiration comes from within your Faculty, and it's the only way to use the Conduit to receive greater intelligent energy that is, and fills, the universe.

⏱ *There's something about you...*

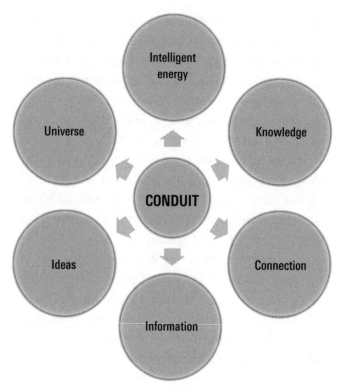

Conduit connects your Faculty to everything outside yourself

YOUR TRUESELF POWER

The TrueSelf is who you really are. Your power, the universe, and your connection to it are part of it. It's your life force and gives you the ability to create the life you want to live. Knowing the unconscious mind is your channel to everything outside of you means you can change your circumstances by changing your internal self.

As your TrueSelf you learn to get out of your own way and reveal an amazing life of love, success, and happiness; realizing and then giving your gifts and talents, in love, to the world. Then you get rewards in full proportion to how you live your life as your TrueSelf. It's how things are supposed to be – it's your default setting. Everything else is just an illusion, and you have been the illusionist. What have you been thinking, feeling, emoting, saying, and doing in order to stop this natural way of life for you? How, until now, has 'stuff' got in the way of your TrueSelf?

You have to trust in something – your guts, your destiny, life, karma, whatever. This approach has NEVER let me down, and it has made all the difference in my life… and don't let the noise of others' opinions drown out your inner voice. And most of all, have the courage to follow your heart and intuition. They somehow already know what you truly want to become. Everything else is secondary.
STEVE JOBS, CO-FOUNDER OF APPLE AND PIXAR

The four characteristics of TrueSelf raise you up. When you are in your TrueSelf, you live your Truth. Through that Truth you travel the Journey that is right for you and as yourself, which means you can better and more easily access your Faculty, doing amazing things as your norm. Being in this place creates a Conduit to infinite intelligent energy. When you're tuned in to your TrueSelf you can, in faith, say that all things are possible.

🕐 *Your TrueSelf is your Conduit*
to the universe.

0–10 YOUR MOMENTS
· ·

Intuition guides and reveals opportunities for you. When you follow your TrueSelf you will, as surely as night follows day, release your inner genius. Think about it the next time you have an intuitive 'knowing' or are in what you used to call 'the zone.' Can you hold that space and just see what happens? What if you could be in the 'zone' more of the time? What then? What difference would it make in your life right now? Dare you take action from the messages that come?

🕐 *Nurture your intuitive ideas and*
thoughts as you would a baby.

PART
II

CHANNELING
CHANGE

*If you're going to do this thing called
life you might as well do it as yourself,
your TrueSelf.*

CHAPTER 7

Moments Change
Your World

'My laces always seem frayed,' Peter told me when we met to discuss setting Standards. 'I've been in business for 30 years and during that time I've had some good times and some bad ones... but, sometimes, when I don't gain a client or a contract, I just can't help looking down at my shoes and wondering if that's the reason why. No one has ever commented, but there's no way of telling how much my shoelaces affect things because no one actually says: "Hey, you didn't get the business because we took into account the quality of your shoelaces and it might mean that you don't pay attention to detail." They just don't give you the business.'

Do you know what an aglet is? It's the small plastic or metal sheath at the ends of your shoelaces that keeps the threads from fraying. As with the retro-reflective cat's eyes, billions of them are made annually. There will always be a demand for them. When I talked to Peter that day, our first focus wasn't aglets – Peter only raised the state of his laces as an afterthought – instead we talked about setting new, higher Standards in all the important areas of his life. Standards that were true to him and his business, but – in his case – it was literally his laces that were his undoing. While some people would look at him and take into account his words, actions, and appearance and make a judgment, others wouldn't do business with him because they would see incongruence. Some would wonder why he had frayed shoelaces. It could mean that he didn't pay attention to detail, or that he didn't care, or maybe that something wasn't all that it seemed. Others wouldn't be thinking about him consciously at all: they would only pick up on this incongruence unconsciously and just feel that they didn't 'buy' him. Yet others would pick up – consciously or unconsciously – his unconscious behavior in trying to hide his shoes.

Even though lots of people had no idea about Peter's shoelaces, he did. So did this small thing lose him some business? Probably, because even if the potential client hadn't noticed and wasn't thinking about Peter's frayed shoelaces, Peter was, and this seemingly insignificant detail unconsciously affected his behavior, self-esteem, and attitude. Hence he was affected and couldn't give his best. His sales ability, his business, and his actual income were impacted because his shoelaces were always on his mind. For just a few dollars, he purchased new shoelaces for all of his shoes. The fact is that everything affects everything else, so Peter understood and felt the knock-on effect of this one apparently 'small' Standard. Since buying new shoelaces for all his shoes he is doing very well, very well indeed.

🕛 *Set new standards and they will*
make room for you.

WHERE DO STANDARDS COME FROM?

As my daughter Dominique wisely told me recently, 'Little things make up your life.' She is so right and, in the same way, Standards influence every part of our lives from the smallest to the biggest: from health to big business and world issues. Setting higher Standards influences yourself, your community, and your outcome – one day at a time and immediately. It's all too easy to adopt or inherit your Standards, but 'knowing your Standards' and where they came from can change every part of your world. First, let's consider where Standards begin and how they are different from goals.

For most people, Standards start in childhood, as parents teach their children how to sit, how to hold a knife and fork, how to speak correctly, Standards of behavior around other children, how to behave when visiting other people, and so on. Children get it. You may never have used the word Standards with them, but rules, qualities, levels, and criteria guide children's behaviors and are set by their carers or parents. But not long after starting formal education, parents and teachers start talking about goals; about attaining something outside of them, instead of looking inside themselves; about conforming to be like everyone else – children quickly develop low self-esteem issues if they think they aren't like everyone else. We are all unique, but we don't celebrate our differences. We all have different ideals and qualities, but most educational establishments in most countries desire to churn out 'sameness,' the homogenization of our children. Fewer children would have 'issues' if we let them learn about and be themselves, and encourage their heterogeneity by showing them how to discover and use their talents. Instead, when they reach adulthood they, like most of us, have to unpack what school and society drummed into them and realize themselves for real. *Vive la difference!*

The setting of personal Standards leads to introspection, causing the child to constantly look inside to discover who they are. This is the start of the Journey to the discovery of the child's TrueSelf. Instead we sow the doubt that the child isn't good enough as themselves, and they must reach such and such a thing or place in order to be successful and better accepted by the world. Parents move their focus from the inside growth of a child to external motivations where the child is constantly measuring him- or herself against others. This is a sure road to unhappiness, low self-esteem, and the psychotherapist's couch.

⏱ What if I could?

PERSISTENCE IN NONSELF KILLS YOU ON THE INSIDE

A family member shared with me how his persistence in trying to achieve the wrong goals nearly killed him. He had set out his goals many years before, and was so determined to achieve them he forgot who he was. In fact, those goals weren't even his anymore, but it took a nervous breakdown for him to realize this. 'It was a trick, a ruse, which caused me stress and huge personal instability,' he explained. 'In going for goals, the achievement of which wouldn't have made me happy because I was miserable along the way. I wouldn't quit, but that persistent pushing against that wall nearly killed me. I thought having goals would bring me success and happiness, but it's how you live each day that counts isn't it?'

'Yes,' I replied. 'Maybe there is no wall, it's about just *being*. As our TrueSelf we become what satisfies us; that inner contentment means that there literally is no wall for us.'

Be your TrueSelf for yourself and you will be better able to serve others – helping, teaching, serving – and you will also be rewarded unconditionally.

There's another way to look at things. Some goals are important for self-preservation – getting food, the continuation of the genetic lineage, and so on. These are natural, instinctive goals, and we don't have to think about them. But we take goals too far. Chasing illusory goals and conforming to the 'norm' causes millions of adults and children to spend much of their lives looking for something that isn't real to them, neglecting what is real and spending their lives trying to find out who they really are and why they are here.

Too many men and women in business allow their customers or their organizations to run them ragged for the 'mighty dollar,' and they effectively sell out their core and their values. This is clearly not conducive to personal success and happiness, and it won't get your inner genius out into your life. Many people fear criticism too. If you suffer from this malady, then remind yourself that you're no longer a teenager, with the requisite angst and peer pressure. If you are just 'You' and live at higher Standards, those higher Standards will serve and suit you.

> ⏱ **Raise the Standards of your**
> **relationships, health and fitness,**
> **contributions, spirit, wealth.**

STANDARDS OF INFLUENCE

And if you don't believe that you conform to society's expectations or are influenced by others' Standards, think about it for a minute. If you live in a place where everyone is expected to be honest, tidy, and polite, you probably will be too. But watch people in a dirty, littered street. They drop litter, too, as people often rely on 'social proof.' Robert Cialdini is Regents' Professor Emeritus of Psychology and Marketing at Arizona State University, and his book *Influence: The Psychology of Persuasion* shares with us the 'click whirr' of human behavior. Social proof is what we notice others doing around us. We use these cues in order to determine what we will do, how we act, and our standards of behavior. The majority of this behavior is unconscious. Look what happens when people can get on a bus without paying. Even people who wouldn't otherwise dream of withholding their fare begin to cheat. You become like those you associate with on a regular basis.

It is such an important issue that we should always, and in all things, consider the importance of the friendships and relationships we keep.

'DROP THE BAD COMPANY'

My brothers and sisters will smile when they read this. 'Drop the bad company' our father was fond of telling us as children, but it always seemed as if he were talking to me. From when we were young children and into our teenage years, Dad always made an assessment of the friends we brought home. When a friend played over my father would treat and engage him civilly, and when it was time for him to leave my father would bid him a cheery goodbye. Then the front door would close and a few minutes later – as if he were computing – would come the judgment. Almost as an aside – like a subtle salesman's 'alternative close' – would either come the dreaded words, 'Derek, don't bring that boy here again' or the hoped-for, 'That's a good boy. He has manners.' The latter verdict meant he could use his other favorite quote, 'You must keep good company.'

Dad, like many parents, could and would make an assessment of our friends. He knew, like a genie or psychic wizard, which of our friends would be good for us, and which might lead us in the wrong direction. When he made that decision it was final. My brothers, sisters, and I then had to summon up the necessary courage and excuse as to why this or that friend was left at the front door never to cross our threshold again.

I didn't realize it then, but my father had a Standard of behavior, manners, and respect that had to be demonstrated by all of our friends. He knew that, without a certain set of

Standards, we might easily fall in with the wrong crowd and, as he loved to say, he wasn't going 'to visit us in prison.' No matter how upset we were with the judgment, the Standard was set.

🕐 **_You will find it easier to be yourself by spending more of your time with others who are on a similar journey._**

Our father was no saint, but for a man who came to England with his parents as a teenage immigrant, with no formal qualifications, worked in factories all his life, lost his wife in his mid-30s, and was left to bring up seven children, he did well, as each of us managed to do well. Standards helped.

From my moment of change I knew to set higher Standards in my acquaintances and friendships. I knew that associating with the wrong type of people would take me down a path that wouldn't serve me. So I subtly cut those relationships. I know that I felt so liberated because I had previously emotionally invested in some associations and wanted to change. I set aside, and gave, more time to people who would directly and indirectly help me to maintain my Standards.

🕐 **_It is how you live by day that determines how you sleep by night._**

FINGER-IN-THE-COLLAR STANDARDS

Unlike a goal, a Standard is a level, rule, quality, criteria, or basis that you set for yourself and adopt immediately, and day-by-day make it unbreachable. You hold on to your new, higher Standards long enough to see what would happen if you did. You set a level and you only act or accept life at that level. It could be as simple as the collar size on your shirt or blouse. Every morning, once I've buttoned the top button on my shirt, I check whether it still fits by putting my index finger in and out of my collar. As long as I can get my finger in and out easily, I'm okay. If I can't, then my Standard is breached. I've probably eaten too much of the wrong food and not exercised enough. Immediately, I do a 10-second check-in with myself, and then take immediate action by upping my exercising and eating a healthy diet *that day*. I also check the fit of my belt. On each of my belts I have two notches. Between those two notches is my range, or Standard. This is my Standard check for physical health.

ABOVE GROUND

I was in Tallinn, Estonia, earlier this year and sat in the square with my friend Edward. I had mentored Edward for part of his career in financial services. We spoke about the previous two years with fondness and counted our blessings. We gave thanks and toasted life.

Two years earlier Edward had come to me because he had been declined life insurance and critical illness cover. This upset him. He was only 41, but he was overweight and had high blood pressure and elevated cholesterol. Edward had witnessed my eating, health, and fitness Standards over the years, so he asked for guidance. When I asked him how he got dressed in the morning, he looked at me askance.

'What do you mean?' he asked. So I explained about the finger in the collar and the belt. Then I asked him what he did when he put on weight. He replied that he just purchased a bigger shirt or suit. We laughed – a lot – but right there and then we discussed and agreed upon some new Standards he could use with immediate effect. These included the right type of eating and exercising.

Edward set down the new Standards and committed to them by the day and each day, one day at a time. After a moment of consideration, he shared something with me that brought a lump to my throat. He said that his new Standards were based on him living a life that would keep him 'above ground,' and he would maintain his new health and fitness Standards in order to see his children grow up and marry, and walk his daughter Michelle down the aisle. In the next year Edward got in shape. We worked in the same building, so I was able to see that transformation. At times I would walk by his office and see him eating greens, salads, nuts, and berries at his desk. Edward now looks and feels the best he has for a long time.

🕐 *Where do you start? You start with a STOP.*

Every single day you exist is compounded onto the next day, week, month, year, and decade. If your body is unfit and doesn't support you, or you become ill and die before your time as a result, it will be largely because of what you did, or didn't do, each and every day with your health and fitness Standards. One day at a time. That's how we get life, and that's how we should live it. Today I could eat a huge pile of fries and drink beer while lying flat on my couch, and I won't die as a result of it. But if I run that regime, living at that Standard or something similar, every single day, then I'm likely to lose my health, and possibly my life, sooner than I'd like.

'Little things' don't only 'make up your life,' they can keep you alive or cause you to check out early. Many people will wait until they are so overweight that they can't get into their clothes! How does your life pan out if that's your personal health and fitness Standard? Life isn't a goal. You can wait until your clothes don't fit or you can agree that your collar and waist size is a Standard that shall not be breached. The old way said get overweight and then set a goal to lose it. Baloney! State your Standards, agree on a level for you, and do the things daily to support and keep that level. It's about daily Standards.

> ⏱ *Your personal health isn't a goal,*
> *it's a daily Standard.*

STANDARDS MAKE GOOD ORGANIZATIONS GREAT

Billionaire philanthropist and broadcaster Oprah Winfrey raised the Standard by creating her own Oprah Winfrey TV Network (OWN), controlling its output, content, and structure. In doing so she and her team set a massively high Standard not seen before in broadcasting. Great companies like Porsche, Walt Disney, Chrysler, and AXA PPP Healthcare use terms in their mission statements like 'Maintaining,' 'Raising,' 'Upholding,' and 'Redefining' respectively, because they are a few of the companies who understand the power of Standards.

These firms realize what it means to their customers, their clients, their employees, and to the bottom line. If an employer treats its employees and business partners with high, mutually beneficial Standards, then those employees are most likely to pass those Standards of treatment on to clients and customers by giving them a high-quality service and product. This is exactly the same principle (of cause and effect) and similar results are obtained in the public or government sectors. Raising Standards in one area affects every other area by way of connection and association. It's easy to raise the Standards of your financial results if you raise the Standards of the integral components of your business or service – employer, employees, customers, products, services, and so on. This doesn't have to cost money, because it begins with a state of mind.

A mission statement doesn't say how and with what attitude individuals should work within an organization.

Once you have Standards set out they can be monitored. What gets monitored becomes accepted by employees and therefore gets done. Having a goal to be a wonderful employer or the public's chosen provider of goods and services won't do what Standards – which engage employees and customers, and give immediate action points and daily behavior checks – will do for an organization.

I act at the Standards that come from my TrueSelf. I am those Standards and I get what comes with those Standards: happiness, success, financial rewards, positive impactful living, and health. What do you want to be today?

0–10 YOUR MOMENTS

Take a moment now and consider the power, confidence, and sense of certainty of that TrueSelf place for you.

Imagine how you will feel when you no longer fear what others think about you, your intentions, and Standards.

Imagine...

- How would you act?

- What would you do?

- What schemes would you originate?

Pause further, and while being fully present consider...

- What have you had enough of?

Standards are in the tiniest details: the unpolished shoes or a tightening waistband. You don't need much money to polish your shoes or change your eating habits, and yet in doing so you make a statement about the Standards you live by. This is how I choose to operate in the world.

Take a few seconds, and contemplate...

- In what areas of your life could you raise or set higher Standards?

- Which of your current Standards is letting you down right now and preventing you from becoming all that you are?

You are the world's puppet unless you take back your strings.

HIGHER STANDARDS CHANGE HISTORY AND THE WORLD

Setting Standards can, in just a few seconds, change your world, or they can change the whole world. For some it might be the aglet on a shoelace, for others it might be about campaigning for human rights, but it's about taking action and not waiting for others to move.

TICKET TO FREEDOM

It was cold in Montgomery, Alabama, on December 1, 1955. A young woman looked up at a man who was asking her to get out of her seat so he could sit down. They were riding on a bus at a time when it was the norm for a person of one skin color to sit at the back of the bus, or to give up their seat if a person of another skin color wanted that seat. Equality and human rights for African Americans had always been a goal. The goal had been held for 300 years. Yet at that moment an event occurred in Montgomery that set alight the civil rights movement and changed the USA and the world forever.

On that day, this young woman said 'Enough,' and decided in those few seconds that she was as good or as bad as everyone else and that as a human being she had a right to keep her seat and sit where she wanted. Rosa Parks had her 10-second moment. It wasn't planned, but in that moment she spontaneously decided that she should be treated by the same Standard as any other fare-paying passenger. Her rights as a human being were no longer a goal; it was her new Standard and so she stayed in her seat.

Rosa Parks was arrested. You see, she had changed inside, but the police needed a little convincing that this was the right Standard for everyone. For this young lady her moment gave her an inspiration that couldn't and wouldn't wait. The moment appeared because the time had come and she took action.

Around the time of Mrs. Park's new Standard, a certain Dr. Martin Luther King Jr. had recently been elected as leader of the Montgomery Improvement Association and knew that 'Injustice anywhere is a threat to justice everywhere.' He picked up on the new Standard and others followed. They boycotted the buses and walked instead, and then they marched. Before long, transport segregation was declared illegal and ratified by the Supreme Court. But the battle wasn't over, because others had to learn the new higher Standard. Eventually though, it won the day. When you set new higher Standards, be patient as you give your world time to catch up to where you now are.

Now Mrs. Rosa Parks will continue to live in history for one reason: In a moment lasting just seconds, she realized who she was and set a new Standard of how she and others should be treated. She then stuck by that Standard long enough to see what would happen if she did.

In April 2011, when I spoke at the Global Speakers Summit (GSS), I made the following statement as part of my concluding remarks: 'In the decade after 1955, via the civil rights movement led by Dr. King, African Americans made more progress toward equality than in the previous three centuries combined...' This was a phrase that came to me as I wrote that talk.

Three months later, I made my first visit to The Martin Luther King Jr. Center in Atlanta, Georgia, USA. I stood with a crowd of other visitors watching a film about the Rosa Parks story. As the narrator concluded he said, 'In the nine years after 1955, African Americans made more progress than in the previous 300 years.' I blinked and shook a bit, and I almost cried.

In November 2008 Barrack Obama set the Standard for black people in the USA and the world even higher when he became the first black US President. I firmly believe that if Rosa Parks hadn't set those Standards all those years ago, igniting the civil rights movement that led to greater equality for black Americans, there would be no Martin Luther King as we know him, and no Barrack Obama in the White House. Standards.

In the late 1980s the German people decided that being separated as a country and kept apart from family and loved ones was an imposed Standard that they could no longer tolerate. One night in 1989 the Berlin Wall came down and, as I write this book, walls are coming down in parts of Africa and in the Arab world; they call it a 'Spring.' New global Standards are being set. Some will try to act at the old Standards, but it's too late for them. Such is the power of Standards.

Martin Luther King Jr., Winston Churchill, Mother Teresa, Muhammad Ali, Florence Nightingale, Mahatma Gandhi, and many other names written in the annals of history knew the power of Standards and used them, and the genius that sprung from TrueSelf, to change the world. You too can make small or great changes by setting Standards that will change you and your world, for now, for good, for ever.

> ⏱ *What if you were in a place where its constraints made it difficult for you to live at your Standards? What then?*

STANDARDS WRITE YOUR STORY

What a story you will have to tell in the future if you, with faith in a positive outcome, take hold of your 10-second moments as they come and live from the Standards that your TrueSelf knows is right for you.

When Rosa Parks set her new Standard she encountered what you too will encounter. Namely that some of the people around you will try to treat you by the old Standard! From TrueSelf comes only love, but you have been in the world for a while, around many people as your NonSelf. They are accustomed to treating you as the old you and by your old Standards. I know that as I expressed and articulated myself anew, I had to be patient with those around me. So will you.

Standards are a *now* experience. You set them and live by them today. Just today, one day at a time. You can't live in the future, because when you get *there* you only have another *now*. *Now* is what you have, so live and be the best of you in the *now*, and you future *nows* will be the greater. Use your *nows*.

You don't have to set Standards with the intention of changing the world. You can just set new Standards that will change you and the lives of those close to you. You might begin with a look at the Standard of the end of your shoelaces and decide to change this very smallest of things. You may do a review of your customers and business or your acquaintances. You might make healthy eating and exercise a Standard. You might put time with your children or family first. Whatever you do is a cause that is set in motion by your new *internal* Standards that will change you *externally*. You will immediately feel better about yourself, which will cause you to be different in yourself, better in your world. The world will begin, for the first time, to see 'You,' and then it will treat you differently and beat a path to your door.

🕐 *Trust and have faith in the process (of change).*

0–10 YOUR MOMENTS
....

The Rosa Parks story thrills me because Standards are everything to me. If you were to do one thing to 'raise' your Standard in one area of your life, what would it be? Then, just do that. As the American author Og Mandino said, 'Today I begin a new life.'

🕐 *This is my perfect day.*

CHAPTER 8

PERFECT Your Standards One Day at a Time

'Divorce, business challenges, and poor health... I was on a downward spiral to disaster. I was just in so much pain. I started drinking heavily and, at that time, I was so far from myself... I started thinking – thinking about my guns... To be honest, I wouldn't be here today if it wasn't for that moment when I decided to set new higher Standards, because that was the key to what I needed.' Kevin, a financial services acquaintance, had heard me speak the previous year and shared with me how, during my keynote, he noticed a shift come over him. He realized that he had been letting his Standards, and therefore himself, slip. The same night he called a close friend, a member of his shooting club, and asked him to take away his guns. 'You saved my life, Derek,' Kevin told me.

I really don't recall exactly what I was thinking the moment when Kevin shared his Journey with me. I do remember that tears came to my eyes. I do recall feeling that my realization was being realized. I do recall a real feeling of love and connectedness. I was honored to help him, but it was actually Kevin who saved his own life because he captured his moment and took a new approach. Changing his Standards brought him immediate change, and took him from potential disaster to a path of happiness and improving health. Since that 10-second moment, he told me, he has stopped drinking heavily, bought a new house, and met a new partner: 'I'm back into my fitness training and martial arts. I have more time with my children. I'm less stressed and my business is doing well. And my doctor can't believe the change in my health.' When you raise your Standards the only place to go is up – you choose to change your trajectory.

⏱ **You are the one that you've been waiting for.**

STANDARDS AS PART OF YOUR PRACTICAL PHILOSOPHY

Although this is a practical philosophy, it doesn't contain thousands of steps in order for you to change. You don't need to do any of that. Change is simple. I have witnessed the lives of men and women whose loved ones and closest friends are their key reasons to find and be their TrueSelf. Regardless of the business and financial success that you attain, nothing, and I do mean nothing, will bring you greater joy than being able to authentically live by your Standards and having greater relationships with your spouse or partner, family, friends, and even clients. Living by the wrong Standards for you will steal your happiness and contentment. Those with money who remain unhappy know this to be true.

🕐 *All riches begin within.*

A 2011 report published by Jae Yang and Paul Trap in *USA Today* surveyed adults with more than $3 million in investable assets. It asked the respondents what consequences they suffered as they built their wealth. Four major areas appeared most often.

Consequence of wealth★	% of respondents experiencing consequence
Not taking enough time off	66%
Not having time for family	49%
Defining self-worth by wealth	31%
Mishandling personal relationships	26%

★ Note: multiple responses allowed

When setting Standards, it's okay to realize that your personal life makes your life. Your life is not incidental. Without the achievement and success in your personal, emotional, health, relationships, and family life, what would be the worth of more money and business 'success'? Woe betide the person who thinks that it's all about the money.

🕐 *At all times, be present.*

Standards are about proclaiming, 'This is *how* I am. This is *who* I am. This is *what* I am,' and sticking to those Standards today, and one day at a time. You don't really know what's going to happen around you as you set new and higher Standards. The best approach is one of high involvement and low attachment. Be fully engaged and stick to your Standards, but let go of any attempt to control the outcome, as you risk slipping into trying too hard and focusing on the future. You're most effective in the now. Think about each day as the only day. This means you can detach from yesterday's anxiety, and, because tomorrow is unwritten, you can let that go too. Our tomorrows will be the very best they can be. And the best way to grow your business or your wealth is to get your inner genius into play today.

🕐 **Be the best you can be today, just today, one day at a time.**

FROM PHILOSOPHY TO WEALTH, SUCCESS, AND HAPPINESS

All humans, of all faiths and cultures, from Mother Teresa to your average five-year-old, appreciate the value of money to some degree. They know it has a use and a purpose. Money can do great good in the right hands, so you'll want to take an approach that allows it to get into the right hands – namely yours, if that is what you desire. To do this you may need to change from what you were doing yesterday. It doesn't have to be a complex or time-consuming process, and is as easy as letting go of your goals and setting higher Standards for your life. From that point, it's about sticking to your new higher Standards, instead of fretting about year-ends and decade-long goals.

What are goals intended to do anyway? They are intended to make you happy and fulfilled aren't they? How's that worked out for you? Are you living out the dream of your potential, or dreaming of living your potential? Setting goals has let most of us down. Goals, by definition, are future-based and can't make you happy today. Now there is a new gold Standard for success and happiness; it is called Standards, and it starts now.

When you look at the tree, the wood appears different.

When you are all that you can be each and every day, success and happiness will be yours because that is what it takes to be successful and happy: Being you, in all your glory, each day. When you realize the power of living as your TrueSelf each day, another goal isn't going to make you anymore 'You' or better at being 'You,' is it? A simpler way is just to be all 'You' can be every minute, every second, every hour, and every day.

When you set Standards to live by, you set your intentions to do only that, and then you will be the change you seek. You won't need a goal because you'll take your steering from your Standards. How will goals make you any happier or more successful if you are already the greatest (and getting better all the time)

'You' in your day? All this works because Standards are a NOW experience. The setting and keeping of Standards keeps you operating in the 'now.' The setting and keeping of high Standards automatically causes you to operate at your finest levels and with your best faculties at play every single day. These are simple laws. They are the same laws that hold the stars in place, which cause an acorn to mature into an oak tree, which power your thoughts and, through causality, allow wealth to flow to you through the application of known principles.

In the minds and hearts of the multitude of self-made, successful people I have met, these laws are more than just theory, and can be utilized by anyone who is willing to suspend the illusion of the world they see and instead make use of this practical philosophy which converts words, thoughts, questions, phrases, and ideas into riches. If increasing your wealth is your intention, then there's no better way to translate that intention than realizing all of your gifts and talents, becoming all you can be, and exchanging those gifts and talents in return for everything you desire in the material world. But you may as well know that the accumulation of money won't be the thing bringing you happiness: Happiness is in the becoming of 'You.' The money is just a bonus. All true success and happiness is nothing more than the outward expression of inner knowledge.

🕐 **Lift up your thoughts and they**
will hold you up.

When I set Standards for my life, they weren't arbitrarily plucked out of the air or taken off the proverbial shelf or from the world at large. That was the old NonSelf way of doing things which got me into trouble in the first place. Taking Standards from just anywhere – from your career, profession, old friends, the media, and the world at large – is generally how we end up living a life that we feel isn't our own. Milton Erickson, the most influential hypnotherapist of the modern era, stated that each of us has a normal (for the individual) healthy core, but it is misshapen and taken on the wrong (for the individual) path by the world around us. He always worked to bring his patients back to their core selves.

Since waking up into my TrueSelf I have noticed that so much happens in my favor: I meet the right people, I get an abundance of opportunities in business and in friendships, and I make a positive difference for others. I know these circumstances and people existed before, but they never collaborated in my favor before, they just never showed up for me. I can conclude, therefore, that nothing changed but me. They didn't change; I did and so they, in effect, altered for me to experience them. I walk the same Earth, but everything is different.

🕐 **Start yourself and everyone on an 'A.'**

0–10 YOUR MOMENTS

As you read through the following chapters, spend some time thinking about your current Standards

151

and where they came from. Did you set them, inherit them, or have them thrust on you? Do they serve you now? Do they lead you to discover more of your TrueSelf? When my moment arrived it was no coincidence that my TrueSelf conveyed to me three little gems:

1. Stop living in the future, always thinking, 'One day!'
2. Reset to Standards of your own making for personal happiness.
3. Living as NonSelf produces unhappiness; TrueSelf brings happiness.

You and I are the same in this respect. No matter what the miles or culture separating us, we are connected by something, something much bigger. Setting and living by Standards makes us realize who we have become and who we truly are; it mends and it makes amends. Living by Standards is the most practical key to keeping you true to yourself, because it causes you to live from who you are and keeps you checking in – questioning why, what, when, who, and how – with you.

Being aware and connecting with your unconscious, as you set and live your Standards, is how you get to spend more of your time in TrueSelf. From TrueSelf you are on the right Journey for you; you are being your Truth, your right of entry to your greater Faculty, and the Conduit linking you to something greater than yourself.

As long as you set your Standards from that centered, balanced TrueSelf place inside, even if you have only now stepped onto that path, you will revolutionize your way of life. Standards can be a tool that allows you to make the change that you want to see in your world. As a consequence you get the opportunity to:

- Have new Standards that truly serve you.

- Set higher Standards in line with your true powers and abilities and based on who you are inside. Allow them to flow.

- Immediately notice the benefits of living by daily Standards.

- Live at your best in the now.

- Recognize where some of your old Standards came from and the traps of NonSelf.

- Have a practical and simple way to live your life as you.

PERFECT LIFE STANDARDS SYSTEM (PLSS)

When I set my Standards, I didn't want to end up 'happy' but penniless and on the street with my family. Taking a balanced approach is important, but don't seek anyone else's counsel or advice. You already know yourself better than anyone else, so ignore anyone else's guesses about what will be 'right' for you. Living by daily Standards is not about being perfect. No one is perfect; it's about living the life best for you, based upon who you truly are.

The seven key areas are listed below, and these affect everything else in your life. The PERFECT Life Standards System (PLSS) focuses on setting Standards as a 'now' experience, which means that they are a now activity. They are not for setting and forgetting (like most people's goals, only revisited at year-end).

⏱ *Act now!*

Personal Health and Fitness

Health brings freedoms until it ebbs or is taken away. Be specific in setting your Standards. How often do you exercise and for how long? Do you eat a healthy diet? Do you have unhealthy habits you need to curb or quit? Are these Standards part of your TrueSelf? What does your inner voice tell you – honestly – about your personal health and fitness?

Recall the 'finger in a collar' story in the previous chapter and the consequences of not having daily Standards in your health and fitness. Every small thing you do affects everything else. Start small, each day, and from that your personal health and fitness will grow. Live with the intention of staying above ground. Your unconscious knows how to heal you as it considers things at change in your life

⏱ *A six-foot sunflower lies within
a small seed.*

Environment

Q: Why is a corn-fed chicken yellow?
A: Simple, it eats yellow corn.

The chicken is bound by the laws of nature to be yellow if it has a diet of yellow corn. Similar laws bind us. Our output is primarily based on what mental food we digest and retain within our system: our external and internal environments.

Your external environment molds you consciously and unconsciously, and if it isn't at a Standard that supports, enriches, and enhances you, then you have the responsibility to change that environment or be potentially ruined by it. What might be around now, affecting you negatively, which you allow in without filtering? Everything matters.

Your internal environment is your attitude, which helps determine what you do, what you're prepared to do, how you respond to circumstances, and your perspective on yourself and life. Whatever internal environment was created in your past, today it is yours and you can choose to take responsibility and control of it.

0–10 YOUR MOMENTS

It's easier to control your environment than you think. Think about the corn-fed chicken metaphor then pause to consider the internal and external environments you create for yourself.

Do you catch a news program on the hour?

Do you wake up to the sound of the radio or TV dumping whatever it chooses into your life?

Do you trawl the Internet for bad news stories?

Do you engage in depressing conversations about the weather, the recent murder, the parlous state of the economy, the riots, the government, what a celebrity got up to with drugs, or which one died and how sad it is?

Is your journey to and from work each day spent listening to or reading the news?

Do you join or start negative gossip and relish in the latest backstabbing?

If you answer 'Yes' to any of the above, then your day consists of allowing in whatever the world wants to throw at you, and you'll be adversely affected without realizing it. You become what you think about. Turn off the TV; tune out of the conversations; don't read, watch, or listen to the negative garbage in the media or – just like the chicken, blissfully unaware of what it's being fed – the color of your life will be based on what you allowed into it.

What is the quality of your self-talk? You come from the inside out.

⏱ *You connect with that which*
you give energy to.

Most people understand the importance of having the right attitude, even if they don't utilize its power. It's sufficient to say that if you don't have a positive mental attitude your life will be all the more difficult: Your joy will be diminished and you'll be more prone to failure than someone with a naturally, or constructed, positive mental attitude. If you feel this aspect is lacking in you, you might find that reading simple and classic books such as *Success through a Positive Mental Attitude* by Napoleon Hill and *The Power of Positive Thinking* by Norman Vincent Peale can help improve your internal environment.

Take responsibility by setting Standards that reinforce your new position, and nourish your heart and mind by setting the very highest Standards of what you allow in and what you create inside. Don't be like the corn-fed chicken.

🕑 *I am not what I think I am.*
But what I think,
I am.

Relationships

One of the world's leading experts on relationships and the author of *Men Are from Mars, Women Are from Venus*, Dr. John Gray says that 'relationships are all about Standards.' The right relationships are a blessing. The wrong ones keep or bring you down, keeping you in a state of NonSelf. No relationship, person, or organization is perfect, but consider what are the best relationships for your emotional, mental, and spiritual well-being. You have to get along with others, but how many people sell out to the wrong relationships and keep them out of some sense of obligation? You only have one life and it's your own.

You'll recognize the wrong type of relationship if you remember your actual deeper feelings when you're around a particular person or organization. This could be a client, a customer, a supplier, a friend, or your partner. A lot of the time, you make do and put up with the person, while all the time feeling negative and disturbed by the relationship.

If you have a career or job where you can choose your clients or colleagues, then choose. My TrueSelf didn't guide me to be a hermit; however, it did guide me to be authentic with other people. Consequently, all the relationships I *did* maintain improved. My business took a quantum leap and my effectiveness increased immediately. I was happier, so I was better at what I did for and with my clients.

As you set high Standards and stick to them, you'll notice some of the negative people around you notice your shift and try to 'help' you, perhaps by telling you not to aim so high. They might mask their words, saying that they are only trying to be helpful, or 'watching your back.' A lot of their language means, 'We don't want you to reach too high, you might fall – or fly.' These deluded folk have nothing better to do than to pull you off track, keeping you somewhere with them – lost.

0–10 YOUR MOMENTS

In the same way our father used to tell us to 'Drop the bad company' and 'Keep good company,' consider your relationships:

Who are your friends and associates?

Who are you walking with?

Where are they leading you?

Is there anyone who, while not a 'bad' person, you might consider 'bad' for you?

Do you have any 'bad' company? What are their Standards?

Which people could you connect with and bring into your life who will help you to stick to your Standards?

Where and how can you find good company?

🕐 *Once you set a new Standard, just 'act at it.' Don't tell anyone; let them see.*

Family

I set Standards to develop and maintain quality relationships with my wife and children. Standards that I shared with you earlier in the book became my core guide that many of my other Standards had to complement or emanate from. Family became the key criteria by which I checked and set everything else. The Standards I set in this area meant that I would have more time – mentally, emotionally, and physically – with them no matter what. Most of us can manage without the extra earnings if necessary, but you can't get that time back with your loved ones.

🕙 *I'm going back to where I belong.*

Emotions

You do know that you do your emotions, and they don't do you, right? This puts you in charge and means you can set and live by positive, empowering emotions. Since your habits are your key drivers, what are the Standard emotions that you 'do' each day? If your Standard range of emotions is limited to the lowest vibration and energy, you won't be operating at your highest level.

🕙 **Your energy is different based upon different associations.**

Depending on where you are in your life, happiness, and success, you may not want to hear that. In the depths of my despair I was blessed to have a 10-second moment, when my TrueSelf clearly said, 'You're responsible. Stop doing what you're doing, and do what serves and honors you.' The absolute wonder of that statement is that if you take responsibility for your emotions, then you can set and live by a different set of daily emotions as Standard. You can set your day with the right emotions when you look in the mirror in the morning. You can choose apposite emotions and practice those emotions as you would any other skill. At one time, I could do 'clinical unhappiness' really easily. Right now I wouldn't have a clue how to, as I set new Standard emotions to live by and they changed me. I fed them and now they feed me. Anyone who thinks that I don't face challenges is unrealistic or dreaming – of course I do. The difference is that my Standard emotional responses are so imbedded that I can handle almost every situation with a positive emotion and act from that place as Standard.

If your Standard responses to life's situations and challenges are fear, worry, or hate, then you should explore where your box of Standard emotions comes from. Ask yourself: How do you respond when another car driver is reckless or inconsiderate? What is your response to problems at work, an irate customer, an aggressive co-worker, or a frustrating spouse? What is it you do? If this were automated and unchangeable, then everyone would be and do the same. They don't.

Years ago, when I lived as NonSelf, I fell asleep most nights doing fear, worry, indecision, and frustration. What is your Standard emotion as you lay down to sleep? What is it when you wake up? Is everyday a 'Monday morning' day? If so, how are you doing that? What do you say and feel, each morning when you make eye contact with yourself in the mirror? Do you look yourself in the eye regularly?

🕐 Who do you need to forgive?

We're all the same, inasmuch as we identify with and reflect one another's emotions. This is because we're part of the same entity. Yet we are fundamentally different, so what has an effect on your feelings may not have the same effect on someone else's. Using the following exercise you can choose to find and set new and empowering positive emotions for yourself, and make them your Standard daily emotions.

0–10 YOUR MOMENTS

Pause for a moment – it doesn't matter whether you're at home, on a work break, on the beach, on a train, or an airplane.

List the Standard positive emotions that you use most regularly.

Now list the Standard negative emotions that you run most regularly.

Which list is longer?

Which list has the most intense emotions?

How wide is your emotional vocabulary?

Make a list of as many positive emotions as you can think of and, as you write, spend 10 seconds feeling and experiencing each emotion. You can repeat this at any time and in any place you wish. A great time to do this exercise, with or without the aid of your journal, is when you feel you're doing your old Standard disempowering, limiting, or negative emotions.

You cannot do or hold a positive and a negative emotion in your body at the same time.

Capture the above idea. One emotion must occupy or take up more time than another in your body and psyche. From now on whenever you find yourself 'doing' a negative emotion, collapse it by overwhelming it with a positive emotion. For this to work or be effective, you must actually get into the positive emotion and be it. With practice your inner self will collapse the negative emotions for you automatically, and your Standard emotional responses will enhance you and keep you on your path.

🕐 *Bring more of your TrueSelf to the party.*

Career

When you change and connect with your Truth inside, you change the way you connect, act, speak, and are perceived by others. When this happens your life is totally changed.

When I set higher career and business Standards it changed the way I operate in business. My model didn't change; I do the same thing but as my inner genius. When you do this, you'll enjoy greater business results, and you can set Standards related to any aspects of your career or business that cause you to feel frustrated or unhappy.

I set Standards that were right for me and still conducive to looking after my clients. I set Standard business hours and even appointment times, but since everyone knew where they stood, it was a win/win for all concerned. I knew from the facial expressions and words of other agents and employees that they knew I had changed. I didn't care what they felt or said because I knew I was becoming happier and, rather bizarrely, better at doing my job and running my practice.

🕐 *Some trip over a pot of gold, yet get up and walk on as if nothing had happened.*

Time

Set your Standards for your life around time; that is, your time on Earth and your time each day. You're here to spend your time discovering and being you. Anything else, regardless of its apparent or material reward, is an illusion, a trick of NonSelf. Time Standards are set in order to simply make what you do and who you are a Standard. You are the guide when it comes to you.

In my old life, the world affected me through my non-choice, through my lack of awareness of externally imposed sets of Standards. My default Standards didn't serve me. I now set Standards deliberately based upon who I really am as a person, from my TrueSelf place inside. In this way I set the course of my life. With this awareness, you will, too.

🕐 *Have you ever let what you think others think about you control your life?*

CREATING YOUR PERFECT LIFE STANDARDS SYSTEM (PLSS)

When you set new, higher Standards in these seven areas, you'll find that they naturally impact every important area of your life. Everything affects everything else.

It's easier to maintain your Standards when those around you recognize you as someone who sticks to their Standards. It's a positive conspiracy. When I started thinking about it, I realized that many parts of my life lacked a defined Standard or contained a quality or level that I didn't set, didn't want, or agree with. Many of these Standards damaged me physically, emotionally, spiritually, and financially, and took me in the wrong direction for me.

The first part of setting new Standards is to consider how your old ones got there. To avoid making the same mistake twice, pay attention to how other people's Standards have unconsciously become your own.

🕐 *I am my TrueSelf.*

As you take time to contemplate your old Standards and write new ones, use the following three steps to write down three of your old Standards and their origins, and three new ones for each of the PERFECT areas. This document will be your PERFECT Life Standards System (PLSS). If you prefer you can download the PLSS document and PERFECT Circle of Standards from **www.derek-mills.com**.

Step 1: Your current Standards

Write down two or three Standards that you run, have, or do in each of the seven PERFECT areas (14–21 in total), then consider the following:

- How, where, or from whom did you get your past Standards?

- How many of your existing Standards did you choose consciously?

- Could it be that your Standards just found you by way of your school, parents, media, society, colleagues, and partners?

- Now some of your existing Standards may serve you, others you may be more than happy with. If so, which ones? What about the others?

- Is it possible that your quality of life, and the way the world perceives you, is based on a set of Standards you didn't choose?

- If so, what Standards would you choose if you rebooted your life and started again today?

- Now ponder the possibility that someone else created the strings that control you. The moment you identify a Standard, or lack of one, in your life, you can change it and live by it.

Note your answers on your PLSS.

Step 2: The source of your old Standards

I call this exercise 'Past Blast,' because it's about finding out what is the 'source' of the Standards you currently run. Start by using or creating a tick chart, like the one shown below. Include all the influences pertinent to your life for each of the Standards: **P**ersonal Health and Fitness, **E**nvironment, **R**elationships, **F**amily, **E**motions, **C**areer, and **T**ime. The more specific you are about where your existing Standards come from, the better.

Source of Standard	The Standards						
	P	**E**	**R**	**F**	**E**	**C**	**T**
School							
Parents							
Sibling(s)/other family							
Partner/Spouse							
Friends							
Educators							
Employer/Business							
Colleagues							
Mentor/Coach							
Media/TV							
Books							
Community							
Church/Religion							
Celebrities							
TrueSelf							

Taking the Standards that you wrote down in Step 1, tick the category you think is most appropriate to the source of each Standard in that area. There can be more than one tick in each row.

You may think that you don't know the source of your current Standards and, if this is the case, become conscious about what levels, rules, criteria, and qualities run your life. Consider your gut feeling for each section, and then tick the box nearest to your response. Don't think too hard. It will come to you now or later. Tick first what comes quickly and easily.

🕐 **Trust yourself.**

Once you know who or what were the sources of your Standards in the seven PERFECT areas, note your answers on your PLSS.

Step 3: New PERFECT Standards

Start by using the TrueSelf exercise on pages 80–81 in Chapter 4. When you're centered and relaxed, bring to mind your best abilities and the people you love deeply. Consider your gifts and your talents. Keep your awareness of the whole room in your peripheral vision. Now, for as long as you like, or can, hold that space. You are present.

As you hold that place, ask yourself the following questions and note down your answers. Whenever you feel yourself thinking too much or your attention wandering, stop, center yourself, and relax again before continuing.

As you go through each question, vividly imagine yourself living and working at your new Standards. As you do this, create a good connection between your feeling and your response to that question. Anchor it into yourself. Intensify the image and feeling of you living by each new Standard.

- What's important to you about **P**ersonal Health and Fitness?

- What's important to you about **E**nvironment (internal and external)?

- What's important to you about **R**elationships?

- What's important to you about **F**amily?

- What's important to you about **E**motions?

- What's important to you about **C**areer?

- What's important to you about **T**ime?

Now rank the answers in each area 1, 2, or 3 (1 being the most important). This exercise is to give you a deeper understanding of what's important to you. The setting of and sticking to new Standards in each of the PERFECT areas will enhance that area of your life to the degree that you set higher Standards and stick to them each day.

Set one to three new Standards in each area. Each Standard must mean something to you, so don't just guess it. This isn't a TV game show, it's your life! Sit now and design and set new higher Standards for each of the seven PERFECT areas. Whatever comes to you from that place, capture it and write it down on your PLSS.

Finally, transfer your new Standards from each area of your PLSS onto the relative section of the PERFECT Circle of Standards, so you have an at-a-glance record of your new Standards.

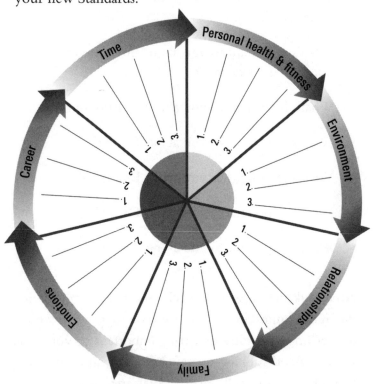

Your 21 PERFECT Circle of Standards

You can choose to live by all 21 of your new Standards immediately, or start with one or two from each segment, adding your other Standards as you go along. The more you stick to your Standards, the more your TrueSelf will be revealed to you. The more of your TrueSelf you reveal, the higher your Standards will rise.

🕐 *The conscious setting and living by*
Standards leaves a lingering imprint
of who you really are.

Buddy up

When, and only when, you have set your new Standards, it's time to share them with one or two people who are the closest to you. These people are your Standard buddies. Children make some of the best buddies, as they are remorseless in making sure you stick to what you said. They'll be around to catch you if you fall or breach your Standards. If you have a good relationship with your spouse or partner, best friend, or colleague, they too can make a great buddy.

You can even have a different buddy for different parts of your PLSS. One buddy might be great for supporting your Personal Health and Fitness, Relationships, and Time, another more supportive of your Career. Even though you're setting Standards from your TrueSelf, from the inside out, having external support around those choices works.

Even with your buddy, avoid deep conversations about the origin or purpose of your Standards. This is the time to 'tell and show.' If you choose your buddy or buddies well, they'll be happy to support you without giving you the third degree, and you can support your buddy far more effectively now because you'll be the real you. As far as the rest of the world is concerned, they'll soon notice when you live out your Standards.

🕐 *When I share, I grow.*

STANDARDS IN BUSINESS SALES

Whatever your business, it necessarily involves sales at some stage. Therefore it's crucial to not only have Standards, but also to draw out your potential clients' Standards and then spend time, honestly and openly, seeing where you can meet each other's expectations. Where they match, it is a hugely significant win/win for everyone. Where they don't, you should both recognize and accept it, and that referral to another person or part of the organization, or another business, is the order of the day. When you begin to think and work 'connectively,' even your apparent 'competitors' can become part of your business solution. Ordinary businesses don't recognize this and, until they do, they will remain ordinary.

One of the ways I increased my new business turnover tenfold was to set and run my business by defined Standards. Just as important to that success was to conceive a system to elicit a potential client's Standards. This is so important, and yet many salespeople miss it and wonder why they don't get the same quantum leap in their results. Knowing your customers' Standards is vital to the sales process: vital for you, yes, but crucial for your clients in order to help them get to their core, where they make great decisions, and then take action from that place. No one else will do this for or with them, so it revolutionizes the relationship.

BEING CONGRUENT

When I'm with clients I go deep into my TrueSelf. I slow down my breathing. I relax and use my peripheral vision. I center myself and tap into my inner genius. From this place I get a sense of the connection with the client(s) in front of me, and let it – based on what comes from my TrueSelf – guide me in the meeting. I follow my intuition in deciding whether to work with someone or not. In the early days, as I practiced trusting my TrueSelf, clients who weren't really for me would slip under my radar. When this happened, without exception, I always ended up regretting taking on that client. In my financial services capacity, I often turn down the opportunity to work with certain multi-millionaire prospective clients. I don't mind the apparent loss of income because I know that this person is just not a client for me; they don't match my Standards or I theirs, and I accept it. Then I am directed to the right clients, and I've done pretty well so far. From that moment in my office when I was laid bare by a question, I knew that this was my life and I should, as much as I humanly can, follow the guidance of my TrueSelf. Having Standards helps.

Knowing your client's Standards gives you the edge

Stelios Haji-Ioannou, the founder of EasyJet, said, 'If you think that safety is expensive, try an accident.' Standards are like safety because they make a difference every day, all the time. Standards are vital to maintain because all breaches cost. If you're in sales, you'll be able to adapt the PERFECT system into your sales process, as I did. To successfully utilize Standards in the sales process you must:

- Identify the client's Standards for your particular area of business. I guarantee that the prospective client wouldn't be sitting with you if they had another organization matching their Standards. They wouldn't leave the other organization and risk losing that Standard of service.

- Help the client identify any past pain of not having their Standards met by a previous supplier of a product or service. The skill is in actually drawing out times where the client's Standards were breached and it negatively affected them. In addition, identify when they've had their Standards met (this tells you how to match that specifically). In asking the client what brought them to the room (i.e., why haven't they taken their business elsewhere?) you give them the opportunity to speak their truth about why they're really here, what happened in the past, and what they expect from you.

- Draw out what having those Standards will mean to the client as they feel themselves moving toward and experiencing those Standards being met, with you in the frame.

- Assist the client in telling you their problem or expectation. Ask for their Standards, so you can prove to them you've identified and can match the service required (if you can) to their Standards of relationship and delivery.

- Demonstrate what your relationship with them will be like, how it will feel, and what you think they'll be saying to you at some point about their satisfaction.

- Meeting a client's Standards generates an extraordinary amount of goodwill. They'll usually be prepared to pay more for your services or products because they know they won't get that quality and the same high Standards elsewhere.

- A skilled salesperson will be able to help the client imagine into the future – how they will feel when you've delivered.

- Find out what success looks like to the client. My team, without exception, always asks a prospective client, 'What would I/we have to understand to ensure we have a successful working relationship?' What comes from that question is gold dust.

Knowing your clients' Standards makes them realize that you understand them in a way that no one else has understood them. This one thing puts you in a place where you can decide whether you want to proceed to do business with them. At all times be honest and true about your Standards and ability to deliver. Be true to yourself, and then decide if the client is for you.

🕐 *When you change the way you look at you, the way others see you changes, too.*

THE NEW VANGUARD OF THE BUSINESS WORLD: STANDARDS

The entrepreneur or small business can focus specifically on achieving more by having high personal Standards – as the aglet example shows – but also by setting high Standards around your product, fees, working environment, and communications. Quality Standards exist in everything from the paper you use to active listening and the words you use. Keeping higher Standards of service allows your clients to see your Standards in action daily, and this changes the whole relationship and makes you congruent to them. What you perceive of yourself is what you project to the outside, so because *perception is projection* you can have the world see you and your business differently. And when the world sees you differently, it treats you and your business differently.

Take Virgin or Apple, for example. These organizations perceive themselves at a higher Standard and project that outward. We, as potential customers, automatically and unconsciously *know* we're going to have a better experience with them because we *know* their Standards. Furthermore, we actually enhance the experience with organizations such as Apple and Virgin because we feel that, just by using their services, we are automatically going to have a better experience. Money can't buy those feelings! Many smaller organizations have yet to grasp this idea of advanced goodwill. How useful would it be to have your customers think and feel this way about your business? Standards affect your psyche, you feel good about the brand and about being connected to it. When your customers feel good about their association with your organization, they associate more with you. This ultimately and positively affects your bottom line.

> ⏱ **Wealth and success is a state of being and proactivity.**

My team and I spend time helping organizations and businesses identify, raise, and uphold Standards that better serve the employer/employees/customer/product/service dynamic. Setting Standards as the vanguard for your business or organization will raise it up. Standards will saturate your organization and then permeate the outside world to your potential customers and clients, your community, and the children in schools (your future clients).

When I talk to businesses I am constantly amazed by how many of them have changed their logo or their corporate colors, and relaunched their brand, yet internally who or what they are hasn't changed. Corporations often spend millions of dollars to essentially look different, but they stay the same in their own minds, their employees' minds, and in the boardroom. Hence, they stay the same in the world. To keep this in mind, remember that the three keys to success in business are the same as in the development of a child: Standards, Self, and Psychology.

1. Know and stick to your Standards.

2. Know your 'Self' (values, ethos, product, or service).

3. Be aware of your business Psychology (how
    your business sees and handles opportunities and
    challenges, how it adds value, and collects rewards.)

Every single day, businesses and their employees grapple
with a multitude of pressures, from staff and customer
relations to the demands of e-mail and telephone calls and
meeting targets. This is a challenge in normal times and in a
financial and consumer crisis it can be overwhelming. This
is why it's vital to have new tools – fresh and emancipating
ways of looking at things – which also ease the pressure and
bring the success you seek in your business, whether you
are its owner or an employee. Have you or your business
fallen behind in your Standards?

THE MARRIOTT WAY

While researching the part of a waiter, British actor Nick
Fletcher did some work experience with Marriott Hotels.
He says that each Marriott hotel runs by virtue of its high
Standards, and every member of staff carries a booklet
called *The Spirit to Serve Basics* and understands the
company Standards. The booklet gives the *basis* for the
whole organization to operate from for that day, one day
at time. There is a different 'basic' for each day, and the
hotel manager can stop any employee and ask them to
recite it. Nick says he learned from this experience that it
was these basics, or Standards, that led to the high level
of professionalism and consistency across all the Marriott
hotels. A business having goals is fine, but maintaining
high daily Standards gets *results*.

🕐 *Where do you start? You start with a STOP.*

NEW YOU

Discovery of TrueSelf, and the use of daily higher Standards, is the new vanguard for inner happiness and outer success. Standards for daily living for the individual or the organization can and will manifest what goals can't because Standards start today and don't stop. Standards create congruence and give Truth to your Journey, so you can live it now using all of your gifts.

0–10 YOUR MOMENTS
....

Your life is more than an exercise lasting a few minutes. If it's worth living, it's worth recording. Your memory will filter and generalize your perception of life and your success. If you want your Truth, you have to capture it in real time. If you haven't already, you might choose to keep a journal on a spreadsheet, an app, online, or up in the cloud. Whichever format suits you best, keep your journal updated. Treat it like a close friend or buddy and share each day. Don't just write down what you've done or achieved, but what you're learning about yourself. Documenting your Standards will show you in the coming days, weeks, months, and years how you've increased your Standards to better suit the person you've become: the magic that happens for you and the moments that change and engage you.

- Each day, record your Journey, encapsulate your Truth, and capture the moments when you access your Faculty and your experience of Conduit.

- Note down your Standards, because you'll need to assess them regularly and check you're maintaining them or whether they need to grow with you.

- Note down the words, thoughts, questions, phrases, and ideas that inspire you and come from your TrueSelf, creating 10-second moments for you.

If you act now as if you're at the Standards that you've set for yourself, then the world around you will conform to create the external reality of whatever you want to be, do, and have as your reality. The world has no choice. The universe wants the very best existence for you, *but you set the standard!* If you have completed this section on Standards and applied them to your life, you already have enough to make an absolute turnaround in the quality of your life. By sticking to the principles outlined, you'll be able to change your life immediately.

0–10 YOUR MOMENTS

On your journey through this book I hope you have begun to realize, or get a glimpse of, who you truly are and what you are capable of. Setting new Standards helps you maintain your TrueSelf and from there everything else flows. Think: 'Today I'm putting on a bigger coat.' As you put on bigger coats you'll shine brighter and brighter. Standards help turn on your inner and creative genius, and it will go to work in and for you. Then, who knows what you may be and reveal. You may already have it within you to be a millionaire or a billionaire, the next world leader, or just the best at whatever you want to excel at. Your path is waiting to be explored.

CHAPTER 9

PERFECT Standards Keep You True

I'm still going inside, raising my Standards, putting on bigger coats – my Standards don't faze me because they come from within. I still look for and experience 10-second moments – they help to keep me in TrueSelf and recognize when I'm stuck. When I think about it, it's usually because I've slipped out of TrueSelf and breached my Standards. This is part of my continuum, my Journey in TrueSelf, and it continues today and every day. Last year I experienced a couple of weeks when it appeared to be a difficult time in my financial services business: Clients seemed a bit tricky and the flow of business seemed like treacle. It was then that I realized the outside world had taken over again. I am watchful for these shifts now because they are vital for recognizing where I am, my Standards, and the space I'm occupying.

Feelings of discomfort, stress, and uncertainty are usually an indication that you're not in TrueSelf often enough. The key is to utilize that recognition of NonSelf as a flag to go back into TrueSelf – turning the apparent negative to a positive steer.

🕐 *You are the genesis of you.*

GUIDEPOSTS ON YOUR JOURNEY

Your Standards are your daily, real world guideposts to come back to when you lose your way. Being human, we're able to understand that, at times, we do lose our way, particularly when we have our first flush of success, when we can forget or misplace the stuff and principles that got us there. At times like this, take time to pause and come back to the Standards that center you. This gives you the chance to catch your breath and move forward as 'You' once more.

I paid too high a price for my 'goals' for almost 20 years. When my life changed I couldn't get a refund. Whatever your past, setting and living by Standards raises your self-esteem and self-respect and, as you do, the world reflects back to you, treating you differently.

Life isn't a bed of roses, but we can massively hamper our Journey and our experience if, for whatever reason, we slip out of TrueSelf. Standards keep you there because they remind you where you're at – the really important stuff. The beauty of this is priceless. So use these opportunities to discover, understand, plan, renew, scheme, and focus. In the drawbacks of NonSelf experiences are the kernels of corresponding opportunities for TrueSelf.

When you act from your TrueSelf you forge authentic relationships. You become congruent with your new higher Standards and that changes everything, your behavior in particular. When you make a decision about who you are and who you're not – particularly if it concerns relationships or business – you immediately become that truer person.

> ⏱ *You become increasingly connected to those with whom you associate regularly.*

0–10 YOUR MOMENTS
....

Choose one area of your life that troubles you and experience it again from your TrueSelf Faculty (what you may previously have called zone, flow, or moments of clarity.)

Now, in this place sit and rehearse that circumstance or issue from the perspective of your TrueSelf space. Hear what you would hear, feel what you would feel. Imagine the power of the TrueSelf's four characteristics being here right now. Your Faculty is here, as is your Conduit to all else, your Truth speaks to you, and you recognize the Journey that you're on. If you do that now, you will literally open the doors to your inner genius.

Finally, as you hold this space, staying centered, make a decision about the issue and set a new Standard around it. Whatever comes to you, stick to that decision, plan, or idea. Commit to it long enough to give yourself an honest chance to see what would happen if you did.

VISUALIZE YOUR STANDARDS

Once you're living to your new Standards, it's important to stay focused on them, so they become part of you. Visualization is one of the most powerful ways to create your Standards as habits. Having set new initial Standards for your PERFECT life, see yourself working and living at those Standards on a regular basis – preferably daily, when you wake and before bed. This is where you get the chance to go deep, identity with yourself, and make changes from the inside out.

Take time to sit and run a movie, or a series of pictures in your mind, of your life experienced at the quality of the higher Standards you've set. The more you do this the quicker you'll internalize and accept yourself at your higher Standards.

I regularly visualize myself in situations where I know my previous Standards let me down or didn't serve me. As I visualize myself in those same situations, I am able to reenact them as the real me. As a result my entire feelings about that experience change, and I see myself literally with a different outcome because I am different.

The following visualizations only take a moment or two each, but in doing them regularly you'll begin to operate without conscious thought, without second-guessing yourself, at your new higher Standards easily and in reality. When this happens everything in your life changes to just the way you want it, quickly.

Visualize one area initially in the seven PERFECT areas and see yourself acting at those Standards in the very next opportunity you think you'll have. Rehearse operating at your new Standards until you actually feel, from the inside out, that this is how you are now. When this is done, move on to the next area of your PLSS. See below for some examples:

Personal Health and Exercise

Visualize eating the right foods and exercising. See, hear, and feel yourself looking and feeling healthier that day.

Environment

See, hear, and feel yourself speaking to yourself in a new way. Run conversations matching your new Standard of self-talk and use words that are congruent with your new Standards. See yourself working and living in a conducive environment for you that day.

Relationships

Visualize being in active, two-way relationships with people with whom you operate at the Standard you've chosen. Create in your mind an empowering relationship connection that you're likely to have that day.

Family

See, hear, and feel yourself spending quality time with your family, and being 'present' with them at all times.

Emotions

Choose several powerfully positive emotions and rehearse your day using only these emotions. Actually see yourself acting out the emotion and being different.

Career

Imagine yourself in client scenarios, or with colleagues, where your approach and Standards philosophy allow everyone a win and you to feel happy. In all scenarios see yourself sticking to your Standards and noticing how people react to you when you do.

Time

This is your time to play. See yourself doing 'you,' as you, whether it's using your unique abilities or discovering and delivering your talents and gifts to the world. Run and mentally rehearse time with your family – the conversations and the fun you'll experience with them. In your career see yourself enjoying your time as you. At times you need do nothing more than center yourself, and consider your talents and how to realize them in the world. Do this just for today, one day at a time.

> ⏱ **Happiness and success are Standards and attitudes that you make yourself.**

Sit and run

You can use this last visualization any time in the day you find yourself in a quiet spot. I still do this in the morning. When I get to the office, I sit in my car with the engine off and visualize the day ahead. I find lunch times are great for this, too. Occasionally I fall asleep, but what a great set of instructions to my unconscious mind while my conscious mind is in abeyance. Priceless!

Run a whole day in your mind as you operating from your new Standards. See yourself in your mind's eye, from your waking moment till you lay down to sleep, living at your new, higher Standards

As you run through the day be mindful to only visualize quality processes. Make sure you're taking the actions, holding the thoughts, feeling the emotions, existing in the environment, and doing the behaviors that match your new Standards.

> ⏱ *Standards are like safety; they make a difference every day.*

Setting and keeping Standards is the power that can make a path where no previous path could be found.

HOW ARE YOU DOING 'YOU' TODAY?

Each day, like today, I endeavor to be the real me. It's now automatic, 24/7. The real me is relaxed, chilled, and natural. I feel content in this place. When I'm around others I often feel as if I'm 'soaking in the people around me,' and just enjoy the connection without thinking about what it might mean. I'm so connected to them. I think it's the 'something' I've got, while I also know that it only works if that 'something' is in everyone else too. Whether they let it shine or not is another matter.

I'm always meeting people who unconsciously feel the connection, too, but can't yet appreciate or define it. It's a sense, an energetic connection. I tune in to people and say whatever comes out. It comes from my gut and I know it's congruent. In the moments when something or someone doesn't feel right, I'm still and quiet; I remain in contemplation. It's really about fine-tuning. The more comfortable I am with trusting it, the more I've realized it's my TrueSelf. I work each day, no matter what I'm doing, to help people give themselves permission and inspiration to be their true selves.

When I'm with clients I don't work with strict structures. Many financial-planning or personal-coaching programs are so rigid and process-driven that they forget there is a human being at the core of it. Life doesn't operate like that. In my meetings with clients I work to feel the point of connection and say and do what is right, looking for the resonance with the client. The more I trust my instincts the better. It seems to create a clearer channel, which I trust, so I work to stay and to coach from that place.

⏱ Practice being centered as your TrueSelf every day.

0–10 YOUR MOMENTS
· ·

Are you checking in? This is like looking in on a friend or neighbor. Just check occasionally that all is okay and as it should be.

At any time throughout your day do a checkup. Center yourself and ask:

1. Is the action or thought I'm about to engage at my new, higher Standards or not?

2. Is the emotion I'm currently holding at my new Standards or not?

3. Is the internal or external environment I'm holding, or surrounded by, serving my new, higher Standards and my TrueSelf or not?

Whatever isn't serving you, be honest with yourself, then decide to shift and stick to your Standards. Eventually this will become automatic and you won't have to do conscious 'check-ins.' This is why, when setting and going through the Standards process, it is vital to choose Standards that mean something to you.

Learn to catch yourself being or not being your Standards, just like catching yourself in NonSelf, and take appropriate action to change that. Celebrate sticking to your Standards (fist pumps are fine, and there's nothing wrong with a leap in the air if there's headroom) and simply change when you find yourself not.

Pay attention to the daily Standards of your self-talk. Opportunities exist most days for you to practice the new Standard of you.

⏱ *Today I begin as my TrueSelf.*

TRUESELF ANALYSIS

If you shake off the shackles of NonSelf what will you become? What differences will that make for your descendants? What is the highest Standard you can set, and what will it take you to maintain it? Then whatever society and others are predicting for you can change for you. If you're a parent, setting Standards will affect your children. Encouraging them to set and maintain daily Standards may reveal an inner path of a teacher, a leader, a media mogul, a healer, a world saver, an ambassador, or a preacher. In the same way that your health is the culmination of your previous daily Standards, your life is comprised of all that has gone before. Your daily Standards, of whatever level or type, keep you in your TrueSelf and affect your current 'now.'

At the end of each month, ask yourself these questions. You might find diarizing your answers helpful to ensure you follow through.

Did I:

- Look out for, create, or capture 10-second moments and take advantage of them?

- Play with the Law of Connection?

- Have extended connections?

- Make more decisions from my gut instinct at a) work, b) play, c) socially?

- Check in with myself each day, consciously being in my TrueSelf space?

- Quit second-guessing myself?

- Stop forcing answers from my brain and pay attention instead to my heart and intuition?

- Really take the time each day to pause and clear my mind?

Have I:

- Formed the habit of recording my creative thoughts?

- Broken or minimized any relationship that is keeping me down, restricting me, or making me unhappy?

- Thought, 'How can I best serve?'

- Remained in harmony with others, especially to strengthen the connection with others who shine?

- Allowed myself to be susceptible to the negative influence of another's 'NonSelf' philosophy?

- Knowingly or willingly behaved against my Truth and wandered off my path?

- Been courageous enough to question 'common' knowledge?

Am I:

- One day at a time, living my life at my Standards, for the good of others and myself?

- Trusting myself to reveal more of who and what I truly am to me, and am I then making that Truth more real in the world?

MONEY DOESN'T MAKE YOU HAPPY, YOU DO
••

I recently met Bill, a very successful entrepreneur who belongs to a particular CEO fraternity. Although he is a multi-millionaire and a well-known figure in his industry, Bill revealed to me that he felt restricted in the organization and virtually whispered that he didn't want to voice his opinion because of what others would think. It had always been that way for him and others. I was compelled to ask why he had never spoken up, and he answered that he didn't want to upset certain cliques. He felt uncomfortable; he knew that things were wrong but didn't want to say the wrong thing. Bill's TrueSelf had been nudging him for a long time. He's an exceptionally creative man and yet he ignores his TrueSelf – his genius. Now here he is, an extremely wealthy man, but unhappy.

🕐 *Wealth is infinite, in an infinite number of ways. How much do you want?*

Some people just let 'things' get in the way of the 'stuff' and spend their lives asking 'How come?' when they're not happy. Wake up. When I need a reminder I ask myself:

- Did I forget to keep looking for and creating 10-second moments?

- Am I so flush with success that I forget to be the TrueSelf that brought that very success out of me?

- Am I 'buddying up'?

- Am I sticking to and reviewing my Standards in light of how much I have grown and changed recently?

- Am I honest with myself about what might be taking me out of TrueSelf into NonSelf?

You can do the small talk, but these are the questions to ponder.

> ⏱ *You don't need to be 'better' or to 'add on.'*
> *Just go deeper, go inside.*

YOU ARE YOUR OWN STANDARD BEARER

The Romans were one of the most successful civilizations in history, and they had a Standard and a Standard bearer for a reason. We all know that neglecting discipline leads to failure. We have to work to maintain our Standards, qualities, levels, or rules. This is how we develop our gifts to the fullest. Some men, women, and children have such low Standards for themselves they fail to realize that almost everything they do in their lives is affected by their Standards. It is how they have set their sail, or it is how they have had their sail set.

Standards are like a thermostat. A thermostat regulates and controls the system and its output. It sets the parameters for a person. Until you change or adjust the thermostat, you limit *you,* your happiness and success. When you change the way you look at things, the things you look at change, too. So when you change the way you see *you,* you change how you treat *you,* and, as a result, the world changes how it sees and treats *you.* It is then that you'll notice how the universe, and the people and things within it, collaborate to help *you.*

🕐 **You can never be what you ought to be until you are who you ought to be.**

Each day you live as TrueSelf, your abilities (your inner genius) and your true essence, as intelligent loving energy, are in the world. Every day that you exist as your TrueSelf, you will witness the rest of the universe conspire to have you be alive with the happiness and the success you came here to experience. Stick to your daily Standards, for persistence has an eternal validity

0–10 YOUR MOMENTS
. . . .

What level have you set your thermostat to? Think about how you could use PERFECT Standards to do, be, and feel what you truly are. There is no maximum setting because you control the dial. What difference can 'being' more your TrueSelf make to your life?

🕐 **You don't pay the price of going on a journey; you pay the price of not going on the journey.**

CHAPTER 10

The Law of Connection

In 2010 I was sitting in my office when I saw an e-mail from the Professional Speaking Association (PSA) with an invitation to attend a local chapter meeting. I'd been receiving similar e-mails ever since Mary Collins, the founder, started sending them to me nine years earlier. In that time, I hadn't responded to a single one. However, this time my TrueSelf guided me to not only read the message but go to the meeting that evening. I followed my intuition and immediately turned off my computer, got my suit jacket, locked my office and drove to the meeting. That night I just happened to get a chair directly behind Peter Roper, the current president of the PSA. As a result of that chance meeting, I spoke at a PSA chapter meeting, which in turn led to a series of life-transforming events, including co-starring in a movie. If I hadn't been in my TrueSelf or ignored its illogical messages, I may not have had the chance to speak internationally or be writing this book right now.

I am thankful to my TrueSelf for, with 'miraculously' perfect timing, guiding me to respond and take action.

What appears as just 'happenings' or coincidences in the traditional sense take on a different meaning. This is the Law of Connection and it is everything and everywhere. The Law of Connection states that you 'are' everything. The key is to recognize that and to connect with it. Then you know that you already have it.

While most people are asleep in NonSelf, I have observed an awakening. I have felt and watched more individuals coming together and becoming their *light* than at any time in my life. My instinct tells me there is a shift taking place among us, and that shift is accelerating. Now is the time to find out who and what you are. Now is the time to reveal to yourself and to the world the gift that is your TrueSelf. Now is the time. In doing so you cause others to wake up and begin to live their lives at a higher level too. More people are awake now than ever before. As more people step into their TrueSelf existence the awakening will continue. I cherish meeting people who are awake or waking. Awake, awake!

TURN ON THE TAP

Many people talk about the Law of Attraction, which is defined as 'like attracts like.' In other words, if you think positive and desirable things they become your experience, and the same is true if you think negative and undesirable things. This description reminds me of a goal – remember those?

A goal tells you that you don't have something – that there is distance in time and space between you and it – so the implicit message is that you don't have the thing. Automatically, the feedback says you and the thing you want are separated. Just like the soccer player on the penalty shoot-out line, part of your psyche and behavior is affected because the Law of Attraction says there is something outside of you that you don't have, but, if you focus on it, you may be able bring it to you, and then will you have it.

Now consider the Law of Connection, which states that you are everything and everything is you. There's no need to attract anything: all you have to do is adjust yourself, like opening a door or turning on a tap, and what is already there pours in. The way to open the door, or to shift the tap, is to get into the Faculty and Conduit of your TrueSelf, which gives access to everything else inside and outside. This is because everything is already around and connected to you. We are the sum of our parts.

⏱ **You can cause a positive revolution when you channel intelligent energy.**

Let me explain. Imagine sitting where you are now and around you is an unlimited number of pipes from every point of the universe (people, things, and knowledge), leading right to you and connecting to you. Each of the pipes has a tap at its end. If you aren't getting what you want in life, you have to *turn the tap* a few degrees and the 'water' pours into your 'room.' The more you turn the tap, the more of whatever that pipe contains and is connected to pours into the room of your life. Notice that, just like the kitchen sink, the water is already in the room, waiting in the pipes. You haven't got to attract it; it's just there. Just turn it on. When you do this your life completely changes. All resources are 'available' to you through TrueSelf, and you can tap into them and realize the life of your dreams.

The Law of Attraction is a linguistic and metaphorical mismatch, which causes many people to think about it and try to use and feel it in a less-than-useful way. If you have to attract something then it presupposes you haven't got it, which is why you have to attract it. There is a difference between you and it. Part of the difference is in time. The language here is relevant because of your linguistic programming. The second part of this law metaphorically uses the language of magnetism – two magnets attract, one to the other, even though they are separate. A better way of considering this might be to think of the magnets as already connected to one another because they are (magnetism, like gravity, you, me, and everything else is energy), and therefore when they are positioned correctly (like turning a tap) one is instantly open and availed to the other directly. It is this existing connection that enables one to utilize the other. If we use the Law of (existing) Connection then we are linked via the pipes of connection. Consequently, everything is already there.

If you're a firm Law of Attraction thinker, fine, simply use the Law of Connection as a tool in your philosophical or metaphysical armory. However, it's worth considering the poorest children born in Africa, Asia, or South America. Did they attract the parlous state into which they were born? No, I don't think so at all. I don't know why some are born into such a state or at such a time, while others are born into wealth and freedom. This is a mystery, but I do think that all energies come here for some form of self-expression and experience. We are energy beings in physical form. History has witnessed many people who broke the bonds of hopelessness, and did so by tapping into something greater inside of them and, in my view, also outside of them. This something guides individuals to lead people out of slavery, to bring healing, wondrous inventions, or scientific or creative advancements. Whatever state you're in, you have the best opportunity to get out of that state by tapping into your best Faculty and the universe. When we remember that we're all connected, with each other and everything outside, this type of thinking brings empathy and accelerates healing throughout the world.

The Law of Connection is immediate. You already are and have whatever you desire to be, do, and have, but you must take action, not just sit there attracting. The action is to become and act from TrueSelf. This is how you turn on the tap. This isn't a passive philosophy; there are clues all around you. You do your part and the rest is waiting for you. We are all the single entity connectively called 'intelligent energy.'

⏱ *Be ready, as you become you.*

ONE UNIFIED FIELD OF ENERGY

We are all energy beings. Science tells us that energy can't be created or destroyed, so we have always been 'here' in one form or another. Everything that we are is intelligent energy – energy that has will and power. There is only one energy field, and even though that energy can take different forms and exist in different states, it remains energy and it remains one. Quantum physicists tell us there is no gap between where one form of energy stops and another starts. There is simply a change of state as another form of energy fills the interspaces, even when that energy is nothing, neither more nor less than gravity or light. No gaps, so everything is connected energy. We're part of that energy and part of everything that is. We are one connected entity. As intelligent directive beings, we are hence all energetically and spiritually connected, one with all others. This being the case, we're in constant community and communication with one another.

The constructed world works to distract us from our oneness. If we pay too much attention to these distractions we forget that we're connected. We forget our oneness, we forget that we're all the same energy, and are drawn into individualism – ego, materialism, greed, etc. – and at worst, dissipate into warring factions. When we're in disconnect, we begin to harm one another.

The unified field has been discussed and dissected, academically and experientially, by the greatest minds in science and quantum mechanics. Einstein, Bohr, Heisenberg, Schrodinger, and of course Max Planck have all described the four characteristics of this 'intelligent energy' or 'thinking stuff' as gravity, electromagnetism, the strong interaction, and the weak interaction. Each characteristic demonstrates that all particles are non-locally interconnected and there is no way for anything (energy/matter) to be separate.

🕐 *You are part of the stuff of life.*

Planck theorized that each energy molecule radiates 'quanta,' or energy elements, and each quantum is proportional to its frequency. As far as we're concerned this means that energy appears to match and react to other states of energy based upon its frequency. As we're all energy, and the laws are universal, it must be the same for us. When we act at a certain energetic frequency with our thoughts, feelings, and intentions, we naturally resonate and connect with other energies at the same frequency.

Quantum physicists, to demonstrate this non-local interconnection, have carried out experiments to prove this theory. In one experiment, two particles were separated by hundreds of miles, yet were observed to react with one another. When one particle was put into motion, say by spinning it one way, the other reacted counter to it, as if it were physically connected. There must, of course, be a bond between the two for one to have that constant reaction with the other. We don't know what the connection is or how it works, but we can witness it in the four characteristics of intelligent energy. There exists a bond or Conduit between all things and us.

This bond is physical and spiritual. We don't necessarily have to understand the mechanics of that connection to be able to utilize its power.

When I listen to quantum physics discourse, I find myself listening to the same words, yet moving from a scientific view to a spiritual view. The words and language are very similar. The action and interaction, and the non-localized connection of infinitesimally tiny bits of matter – whichever one they discover next in the Small Hadron Collider and the Large Hadron Collider – takes me into the spiritual world and leads me to think of God, the universe, and our spirits as being one, with no beginning and no end to us. For me the circle is complete; the smallest is also the greatest and the greatest is also the smallest, as one.

⏱ *If you had all of the resources and connections in the universe at your disposal, what would you do?*

WE ARE ONE BODY

The body is one unit, one entity; all parts supporting the others. The heart pumps blood to the brain and all the major organs, the feet carry the hands to work, all in symphony and to mutual benefit. The left hand would never take a gun and shoot the right hand because it knows that it would only be harming itself. The organs and cellular levels of our bodies know they occupy an interdependent world and depend upon each part supporting the other through the connection and the intelligence that each cell carries. Notice how your feet respond in milliseconds to your outstretched hand reaching for an object outside of its reach, and walk the body toward the object on behalf of the hand. The stomach shares its food with all the extremities of the body, and the blood regulates the body's temperature and manages demands when under pressure. All this activity is for the common good; and all the individual parts use an intelligent connectivity for a common purpose.

A 20-YEAR LOOP

It was June 2010 and I was standing in a room of professional speakers about to deliver the first talk of my speaking career (outside of financial services) in 20 years. It was my first speech on Standards, and the group would formally assess my skills and give me feedback. It was an important moment in my life and I knew it. I centered myself and began, but as I got to the part of my story where I mention the Dale Carnegie course and the wonderful people I met, I saw Phil Ryan sitting in the front row. He and his wife, Jill, were the lead instructors on my course 20 years previously. I hadn't seen Phil since, and yet there he was in the same room at the moment that would make or break my professional speaking career! I was flabbergasted.

Phil and I had a brief catch-up conversation – for the benefit of the rather fastidious timekeeper that evening – which is why I went two minutes over.

Ahem. Phil said that he remembered me. Of all the places and times that I could have chosen, it was in that time and at that place. What shook and moved me almost to tears was when I received an e-mail from Phil the next day, which said that Jill remembered me, too, and recounted to Phil the story that I had told, 20 years earlier, of my mother's death when I was 13. The circumstances of my talk, the events leading up to it, and the contents of that e-mail were a clear message to me that my life had turned completely around and I was ready for my greater Journey.

🕐 *Always seek people who are operating*
from TrueSelf, and have them in your
life by strengthening the connection that
exists through our unified field.

There is an 'intelligent energy' that *is* you, me, and everything and of which we are a part. This intelligent energy expresses itself in, with, and through each of us and everything else because it saturates everything and is everything. Each of us has access to the intelligent energy and we regularly receive moments that, if acted on, have life-changing results. These doorways to greater self have always been there, and always will be. But most people have no awareness of them, and many of those who do get a glimpse of a door keep it shut, either by neglect or by default. When you open the door and take the Journey to your TrueSelf, those around you will begin to say that you have a certain 'something.'

I know you're ready for some answers because on this wonderful day above ground, while there are many other things you could be doing, you're reading this book, seeking your Truth. When you are your TrueSelf, there's no limit to what you could be, then do, then have.

⏱ *Think about it... everything that you have ever learned is within you as a resource.*

FEED IT AND THEN IT SUSTAINS YOU

I use words, thoughts, questions, phrases, and ideas to go into my centered TrueSelf space much of the time. It's also just a place to be, just like a speed-meditation. I have been there so many times that the world now automatically supports me in getting into and staying in that place. This is key. When your world supports you in getting and staying in your TrueSelf, the world is your oyster. Stay in that place so you can access your inner genius as and when you need to. As you do this, over time you'll begin to notice that positive serendipity becomes your norm. Tiny and massive connections will be your common experience, along with apparent 'coincidences,' which I call 'co-inside-ences,' because there's no such thing as coincidence. When the hand wipes the brow or the feet support the body, this isn't a coincidence, because they are connected and part of the same. Therefore, when you're in harmony and one part of the universe supports the other, you shouldn't be surprised either.

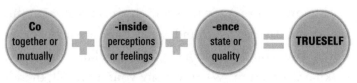

Connections create co-inside-ence

THE WAYS THE WIND BLOWS

Not all of my experiences have been huge, but they've all been significant examples of the Law of Connection at work. A couple of years ago I decided to begin recycling instead of simply paying lip service to being green. Last spring, as I sat at home, I had a real sense of knowing that I had to take the whole environmental thing much more seriously. In that moment I set new Standards in relation to the type and amount of household garbage that I would recycle. I even knew the type of recycling container we needed and where we should place it. Eureka. I was still holding these thoughts as I got in my car to pop to the local store to pick up some groceries.

It was a very windy day and after a couple of minutes driving, I spotted a green cylindrical thing being blown up the hill toward me. As this point my eyes widened in disbelief (hey, I'm only human). Then, as I pulled up at the stop sign, the object was blown to rest against my car. My jaw dropped open. Without even having to step out of my car, I leaned out and picked up my new recycling container, and drove on my way. My wife and children laughed when I recounted my story. You may laugh, too, but that one incident is one of the simplest and purest forms of my connectivity to everything. It would appear that the universe has a sense of humor. No one directs the wind, yet the wind carried its solution to me, with the greatest of ease. The links between your TrueSelf and everything else exist and can never be severed, but the line must be open in order for you to receive the communication.

When you experience coincidences and serendipity in your life, this is an indication of being awake and being in TrueSelf. If this isn't your experience, it's an indication you should pause and center yourself, become present and hold TrueSelf as long as you can, as often as you can, and act from that place. Your life will then become full of what appear to be coincidences and amazing happenings and 'little miracles.' You can still be thrilled and enjoy them, even when they become your norm. Your life begins to collaborate in your favor as you join up the dots around you.

Serendipity and coincidence aid and support you, when you let them.

0–10 YOUR MOMENTS

When you go into a room, or on a train, bus, or airplane, sit and imagine the invisible connections between you and everyone nearby – the man opposite or the people in view. Now center yourself and place your attention on the connection to the people behind you, and sit and hold those connections. If you have just entered a room and are in TrueSelf, let your instincts draw you one way or another, and follow that particular 'pull' or guidance.

I've done this many times, and sometimes the benefits are immediate and obvious; at other times I didn't get any immediate apparent benefit. Perhaps, in these moments, I make connections with people who will play a greater or lesser part in my life in the future. In addition, who knows what your connection gives others? What words, thoughts, questions, phrases, or ideas might you share with each other, and what can you each do with that energy? Good can only serve our world in ways that are infinite. Those we connect with will pass on the rewards of that energy to other people. 'Seeing' other people helps them in turn to 'see' others.

🕐 *My most creative outcomes appear as the result of holding my 10-second moments.*

USE THE LAW OF CONNECTION TO SERVE OTHERS

I often think of the 'spirit' of the major religious festivals and anniversaries that we celebrate, whether it's Christmas, Diwali, Eid–ul–Adha, Hanukkah, or other festivals. For instance, consider Christmas or Holiday 'Spirit.' What is that spirit and how does it manifest? The 'spirit' is nothing more than people being relaxed and allowing themselves to be open enough to look for the connection with others: to let themselves be their best and allow positive energy to flow to and from them. Notice how people smile more, are more tolerant, and silently wish each other good intentions. In doing so, we begin to 'see' one another – no gifts or material manipulation is required to do this – as we share the same energy with complete strangers, bidding good intentions to people we may never meet again.

*🕐 **Regularly find someone you feel is lonely and let him or her know that they are not alone.***

Just for a short while we realize that we're all in this together, that there is more than our isolation and we're part of something bigger that is more than ourselves. At other times of the year most people are less bothered about others. I'm not saying that it's right but that's how it is. Soon after any holidays, festivals, or celebrations, notice how the material, workaday world drags you back to the matrix – to what we might call reality – and away from that experience of unified connection, and into NonSelf. At these times, we can continue to share in that spirit with others, and make our energy self-evident, as we continue to do, say, and be the thing that caused the 'spirit' in the first place.

Another way of thinking of your TrueSelf connections is that even if you can't discern what came or comes from a particular connection, the fact that you're in your TrueSelf place is reward enough. When you think back to the moments when you're most connected to others; when your awareness is encompassing; when you have knowledge of yourself; and when your best mental, physical, and emotional powers are at your disposal, you'll practically be living the best life possible. Each time you have an amazing happening, capture that moment and add it to your storehouse, as each will serve you and increase your Faculty.

PERFECT CONNECTIONS

Jane, an old family friend, shared how she experienced a huge internal shift. She and her partner, Stuart, had lived together for many years. They were happy, and she always assumed they would marry one day. She wanted children and being married was important to her. One evening, Jane asked Stuart whether he was ready to settle down and start a family, and he said, 'No, not yet.' In that moment Jane became still and had an inner sense of knowing from deep inside. She had assumed that it would all happen, but then realized that she was waiting for the wrong person and had been forcing the issue and the relationship.

In tears she explained to Stuart what felt right for her and that she loved him but wouldn't be staying around. He protested, but Jane knew that there was someone else out there for her. To the shock of their mutual friends, she left Stuart the following week and went to Europe for a week. Jane sat alone in a restaurant, many miles from home, listening to a pianist as he sang. He called to her, 'What song would you like?' as he'd done to others many times before. From that moment everything changed as she and the pianist, Karl, grew to know each other and fell in love. She went away to get away from everything and, as she says, to 'find herself.' From the moment we met Karl, we all knew that they were perfect for each other. That was 20 years ago, and they are still married and very much in love. Stuart, too, found a new love and is happily married.

⏱ *A lesson of history is that the stuff that people often thought of as imaginary or preposterous, turned out to be real.*

UNKNOWN POSSIBILITIES

Adversity often sparks Conduit and connects your TrueSelf to the world and vice versa. I believe this phenomenon is caused when you resign yourself to the fact that you're not being the real you and that your experience isn't what it could be. Then you're more likely to pause and go looking inside for an answer, or to listen to your inner voice.

My use of the Law of Connection has brought me to this place. Many significant opportunities and gifts, as well as the odd recycling container, have landed in my lap as I have applied this philosophy. Only this morning my assistant advised me that I had received an invitation to speak in India next year. I was excited; I have many Indian friends and it seemed obvious that I would spend time there. The invite was based upon my performance at a talk I did in Chicago earlier in the month. New connections are everywhere.

NEW CONNECTIONS
....

At a conference in Los Angeles recently, I was sitting with some 200 delegates focused on the debate. Across the aisle and on the other side of the room was a person who I felt I had to connect to, although I didn't know why. I'd seen her before at other conferences. From the delegate book I knew her occupation and position, but I didn't have any logical reason or human interest to connect with her. In the latter half of the debate I decided to 'open a channel' to her. While keeping this channel open, I paid attention and listened to the debate. In fact, by the end I was still engrossed in writing notes in my journal and was one of the last in the room. But, as I wrote, I sensed a presence and looked up. There was the very person I had connected with. She smiled and suggested we grab a coffee at the interval. She is a unique person, with an incredible spirit and capacity for love, and is one of the most influential ambassadors for peace in the world. We are now the closest of friends, supporting one another and connecting with each other's families, often with incredible 'co-inside-ences.' My wife, children, and I adore her, and a picture of her is in our home. We've never done business together, but through our trans-Atlantic connection we have a strong, mutually supportive relationship. Everything flows simply and easily when you're in TrueSelf.

🕐 *As you become your TrueSelf, areas and unresolved issues in your life will unconsciously be revisited and resolved properly, by you. As a result you move forward as True You.*

LOOK FOR COHERENT ALIGNMENT

When two people exist at a similar energy or vibration, communication between them becomes easier and causes prolific positive outcomes to their mutual benefit. In this space the two become coherently aligned. In this state they both shine.

We've all experienced losing touch with an old friend or acquaintance and, at some random point, felt the urge to contact them again, only to find they were just thinking about us too. It could be that you were thinking about them and called, only to hear them say, 'Wow, I was just thinking about you!' What's happening here isn't so unusual (inasmuch as they were more accurately *feeling* about you rather than *thinking*). Those few seconds of alignment are an expression of the Law of Connection, and that moment is a consequence of being in coherent alignment with another person.

Coherent alignment is a close energetic or vibrational resonance between two or more people at the same time. This often happens between twins, siblings, and close family members. Take time to explore what this might mean. What is happening in the other person's life and in your life where realigning might prove helpful or beneficial? If nothing else, reestablish the relationship, because the meaning may be revealed in time.

0–10 YOUR MOMENTS

Exploring the moment of enhanced connection between you and another person can be quite revealing. The next time you experience coherent alignment, or if it has recently happened for you, record what you were thinking and doing and, most importantly, what you were feeling – the mood and vibration you were in – at the time. Were you happy and excited, or expectant and open? Feeling curious or adventurous?

Then, and this is important, remember to ask the other person what they were feeling, thinking, and experiencing in that moment. What was happening in their life? What were they embarking on? Do a proper catch-up, but it's also worth exploring a bit deeper, just to satisfy your curiosity about what is happening here and why you realigned at that specific time.

You won't be surprised to discover that your feelings, thoughts, and possibly your circumstances, are similar. The very fact that you connected 'coincidently' across the miles and time was memorable for you both, so you should be able to remember what you were 'doing' at that time. As he or she is your friend, they, too, might be very interested to wonder...

⏱ *Humanity's greatest yearning is to grow and connect.*

It's likely, as you become more of your TrueSelf, that coherent alignments will become more regular, so you'll get the chance to test this theory. There is an important principle of coherent alignment, inasmuch as when two people coherently align, as long as both are shining in their TrueSelf, they collectively give off more light, which means that the growth in their businesses and personal Journeys can be quantum. The worlds of entertainment, science, and business are full of examples of where two individuals came together, more often 'coincidently,' and then went on to become world leaders in their field. When two energies align significantly it's rarely without great opportunity.

Remember when you felt a connection; when you met someone for the first time and you both felt as if you had known each other forever, or that you had met before. Was this just weird or were they a kindred spirit? You 'knew' this person because, in that moment, you were both open spirits and connected. Your sense of familiarity is heightened when you connect to another person because you really do recognize one another. Such moments are of the 10-second-moment variety. This is when you succeed or fail by choosing whether to develop that connection or not. Many times when you can't see the logic in what your TrueSelf is sharing with you, or guiding you to do, have faith because over time, you'll notice that it will never let you down. Trust your TrueSelf intuition rather than the NonSelf world. You can only let yourself down by failing to follow up your internal guidance.

⏱ *Accept the 'stuff.'*

The benefit of following connections is that you get to take action. You get to follow up and follow through with real people; opportunities inevitably follow. You will connect to people and circumstances in line with your intentions. Circumstances will arise which otherwise would never have occurred. Like me, you'll begin to notice that the right people turn to you. They see you. When the world sees you differently it changes the way it treats you. When this happens, everything will change for you because every moment in your TrueSelf is a moment of true creation.

Look for the light in others, and align yourself with others with positive intentions, in a spirit of positive energy and harmony. This approach has created many a freedom and financial fortune in history: Henry Ford, Dale Carnegie, Mahatma Gandhi, Martin Luther King Jr., Lech Walesa, and Nelson Mandela all knew and used the intelligent energy at their disposal when they were in the right space and time.

Maybe even now you can begin to believe that the universe supports you in your endeavors, in what you are and in what you do. The reason for this is simple: In doing so it is doing the best for itself.

TRIPLE PERIPHERAL

When you're in your open TrueSelf state you're notably more receptive to receiving messages from your Faculty and Conduit. In this place you're incredibly resourceful and creative in your output and learning. The Triple Peripheral is one of the most incredible methods of finding and staying in a state of TrueSelf. When I first happened upon it, I found the Triple Peripheral an effective way of getting into my TrueSelf place quicker and easier, and staying there for longer if I was already in that place.

Expanded vision is a common aspect of what we call zone or flow, and also ancient meditations. When you're experiencing any of these, your vision is enhanced and widened from focused, or foveal, vision to peripheral vision. Ordinarily we filter, distort, and generalize our experiences of the world. The mind doesn't let us become aware of every single thing we hear and feel, or we'd be overrun with millions of bits of information. In order to protect you from overload, your mind filters out what it thinks you don't need. It also brings certain sounds, smells, sights, and feelings to your attention if it thinks you need to upgrade your usual mode of being to fight-or-flight mode. When I realized this, I began to play with my other senses.

MY TRUESELF SPACE

I can get into my TrueSelf place by just listening to absolutely everything within my hearing range, from my breathing to the sound of the traffic, the clock in the room – anything I can pick up. In doing this I can get into a meditative state very quickly. I'm aware yet centered, meaning I can interact with the world around me. Similarly, I found that when I ignored my other senses and just focused on my physical feelings, I could feel my buttocks on the chair while sensing the beating of my heart and the feel of my toes in my shoes. When I did this, I always kept my awareness. Nodding off isn't practical if you're in a meeting or presenting. I quickly realized that I could use a combination of any of the three main senses to help get and hold me in my TrueSelf space for longer, while interacting with others and keeping my inner genius in play at the same time.

Triple Peripheral will take and keep you deep into a place that is conducive to operating at and from TrueSelf because it supercharges your awareness. You will massively increase your ability to connect with others and, as a result of being more easily in your TrueSelf, pick up thoughts, ideas, and guidance.

0–10 YOUR MOMENTS

You can go peripheral using any of the three main senses, not just vision. Practice Triple Peripheral when you next walk down a road. Before, you may have walked along without hearing the birds singing, or running water, or even the sound of your footsteps. Many things distract us in life, but it's a great skill to be able to expand and collapse your awareness of TrueSelf and things at will.

As you practice focusing on your senses while remaining aware, focus your thoughts on questions

to your TrueSelf. As you stay in that place – hearing, seeing, and feeling the detail of everything – use all three senses to create yourself in this day, and see yourself living and working at your highest Standards. You can start with your career, a relationship, or family. Having a Triple Peripheral experience, rather than just visualizing it, is a massive enhancement to your ability to make the day real for you.

The Triple Peripheral is essentially 'openness of spirit' via your senses and is a shortcut to centering yourself. Think of the Triple Peripheral as a bridge between being so aware that you're not centered and being so internally centered that you can't interact and direct your world – feeling at bliss while sitting on a hillside won't get you that sale. You can sit or stand and practice the enhanced, interactive awareness of Triple Peripheral any time. You can also utilize any of the three senses to help you hold your 10-second moments. Then, as always, 'listen and follow' the guidance of the words, thoughts, questions, phrases, and ideas that come to and from you from your TrueSelf.

🕑 *This stuff is the juice of life.*

MASTER YOUR MOMENTS; EACH IS THERE TO SERVE YOU

The Law of Connection is a method of receiving messages and guidance from outside of you, as in prayer, by sending enhanced thought waves to the source/creator. Then it's a matter of being still and present in order to receive guidance from within, trusting your inner self and acting on what comes to you. Being in TrueSelf is the best way to utilize the Law of Connection. It's an interactive law, so you're responsible for turning on the tap or opening the door. You know how to do this now.

As you practice recognizing your 10-second moments and being your TrueSelf, consciously look around you and have your radar on. Your TrueSelf is your channel to the universe, and the universe seeks to get your attention with 10-second moments. I trust the Law of Connection to work for my benefit. I allow the Law of Connection to guide me, showing me where I should best sit on a train or even at a dinner table. Occasionally nothing seems to happen, yet at other times I am sitting right next to a person or on a table with them where it becomes obvious to one or both of us that we are just the connection, directly or indirectly, that the other needs at that time.

I appreciate that some of these ideas may be beyond what you're prepared to do or need at this time. If that's so, just utilize what you find most useful and come back to this anytime. The laws affect us whether we're aware of them or not. In reality it doesn't matter what you call the Law of Connection, or even whether you believe in it because, rather like gravity or magnetism, it will work upon and around you regardless. The right business connection, client, partner, or lover could well be in the room, yet you won't see him or her. A person becomes wise by virtue of the fact that they can utilize power without having complete knowledge of that power. Faith in certain laws is one such power.

For example, do you actually know how electricity works? I don't, and neither do many great scientists. They have an idea, but can't tell us conclusively how and why that type of energy does what it does. The current conclusions are theoretical and will last only until someone discovers a better theory. Yet we all utilize the power of electricity to light and power our world. Just like electricity, the Law of Connection will work in your favor, but you have to turn on the light. You are, and forever will be, connected to and part of all that is. The more you realize your gifts in the world via TrueSelf, the more you'll revolutionize your results, because you will be tapping into the very stuff that created and brought you to this mortal plane.

It is by virtue of the Law of Connection that the characteristic of Conduit works, bringing guidance – in words, thoughts, questions, phrases, and ideas – via your intuition to you. You can trust your TrueSelf best to guide you to do what is best for you.

Where there is darkness, be love and light.
In the absence of collective love and
light, the world suffers.

You may not be here to change the world, but you can use this philosophy and its components to change your world. Your world can change in mere seconds, but do you pay attention to which seconds? If you can accept that there is more to you than just you, that you are part of a greater 'something,' and that we are all connected under this law of existence, you'll recognize coherent alignment as an opportunity to hold a 10-second moment and to see what *would* happen when you access your Faculty and the Conduit. It is in these moments that you shape your life.

0–10 YOUR MOMENTS

The Law of Attraction states that there is something outside of you that you 'ask' to come to you. Instead, consider the Law of Connection, which states that you **are** everything. The key is to recognize that and connect with it. The more you utilize and play with the Law of Connection, the more you'll experience little miracles happening to you, and for you, day by day.

🕐 *Collectively and eventually the good will get us.*

CHAPTER 11

Realize[2]

My brother-in-law Andrew went to school with a kid who never paid much attention to what the system was trying to make of him. He wasn't a delinquent or disruptive, he was just away in his dreams. He knew who he was and he had a plan. It didn't matter that no one else could see his vision, as long as he remained true to himself. He wanted to be a hairstylist and starting out wasn't easy, but his intention was to be his absolute best and to give a level of customer service second to none. He opened his first salon in the UK in his hometown of Kidderminster, and success followed quickly with his own brand of products and a chain of salons. In January 2001, having won literally dozens of major awards and international acclaim, he died prematurely of a rare disorder, leaving a legacy of over £2,000,000 and a name that is known throughout the world. His name was Umberto Gianni and he lived his dream.

Umberto realized what he wanted to do and who he was, and then he spent his adult life, short as it was, making that real in the world. The world will forever be a better place for his having lived as he was born, as himself.

I wonder if we were to meet now, face to face, if you could share with me why you are here and how you came to pick up this book. What series of events or thoughts and feelings lead you here? What do you intend to do with what you've gained? What greater happiness and success will you now create? What is success anyway, and how do you know when you're experiencing it?

🕐 **Take what you are and make it what you do.**

SO WHAT IS SUCCESS?

Many have postulated the answer. As for me, I am certain what it is. My intention isn't to interfere with anybody's religious beliefs. I just have a view about what I know and about what I don't.

You may believe that you came into 'be-ing' at the moment of your birth or conception, or that you existed in some form before either of those events. You may have faith that when you shuffle off this mortal coil, you'll exist in another plane – heaven or another place – or as a form of energy. I believe that all of these are true on some level. You may believe something completely different. For the purpose of what I am about to say, it doesn't matter what anyone believes – whatever and wherever you were before you existed and wherever you go when you die – what matters, in this moment, is why you are here in this form now.

I have a belief that we're here on Earth for a reason. Being a simple man I feel that we're on this physical plane, in these bodies, to find out what we have and – in love – to give that which we are and have out to the world.

⏱ *The real opportunity for success lies within the person and not in the job.*

SUCCESS IS REALIZE²

There are two parts to the full answer to the question, 'What is success?' And they're simple. Part one of the answer is Realize and part two of the answer is Realize.

The first Realize is to look within and discover our gifts and talents. This is a lifelong responsibility. The way the universe works, each of us comes here with a part of the universe within us. We're given those gifts, talents, abilities, energy, and love, and we get to spend our life discovering, looking, finding, and realizing what they are. Whether your gifts and talents are the ability to coach, design, help, sell, build, dance, teach, care, resolve, lead, heal, invent, entertain, create, logic, grow, nurture, perform, empathize, sew, understand, research, speak, sing, develop ideas, or write, your first responsibility is to commit your life to discovering that talent. You do this by looking inside yourself, feeling out who you really are and finding out what your 'talents' are while on this Earth. This is the essence of the first Realize.

The second Realize is to literally realize – to give life to or make real in the world – whatever it is that you discover inside you as you travel your path. Why would the true power, intelligent energy, the universe, love (all called God), whatever you believe in, give you these gifts unless you were supposed to get those gifts out into the world, to make real those talents? To realize is to make real what you have inside you outside of you, for the benefit of all mankind now and to come.

Sure, this second Realize takes courage – to dare to be who you really are, and to then be yourself in a world where it's the exception rather than the rule. When we move on from this mortal plane, we'll have a different form, and our expression of the universal intelligent energy will be altogether different. We are here to Realize^2.

⏱ *Why are you here?*

IT IS LIKE COMING HOME

The world's populace may not immediately support you and your attempt to realize, but enough people will give you encouragement, so you can begin to realize your TrueSelf and realize your talents and gifts in the world.

Have you noticed that children have no fear of Realize^2? Ask any group of seven-year-olds who they are and what they want to be, and they'll share their dreams – enthusiastically and noisily. Ask a group of 37-year-olds the same question and you'll be faced with reluctance to even accept the question, never mind give an enthusiastic answer! By 47, most people won't want to discuss or reveal what they feel inside. A lot of this is because we fear criticism and what others might think or say.

> ⏱ **Be excited, like the mind of an eight-year-old.**

The world – created by other people – conditions us to try to satisfy the social norms rather than ourselves, and so most people never realize their greatness. Most lose faith in being *who* they are and spending their lives being their TrueSelf, real in the world. When you have the courage to be yourself you feel comfortable in your own skin, more centered, and it feels like coming home after a long trip away.

The joy of living as your TrueSelf is that at any time and at any age you can stop being the 'You' that you think the world thinks you should be, and begin to live your life based on your lifelong yearnings, desires, and passions. Right now you can begin to Realize.

Realize and Realize are not added together in some logical approach; instead, one is a multiplier of the other. One is to the power of the other, and in return the other is to the power of the one. The more you discover who you are, the more you can make that real in the world, and the more the world will reward you. The more that you make your gifts real in the world, the more opportunity you'll get to determine who you are. You'll notice that the world begins to make room for you, giving you the chance to shine and the space to grow into something greater. Each realization complements the other, which is why your growth and results will accelerate at an exponential rate. One hand washes the other.

🕐 *At all times* be.

WHAT ARE YOU WAITING FOR?

Waiting to discover who you are and what you're capable of, and not having the courage to be who you are, can be a painful venture. One of the most acutely painful times in my life happened when I read in the local paper of a woman who was making an appeal for money to pay toward some life-maintaining equipment. As I sat at home I realized that the amount she wanted was almost exactly what I had in my bank account. I'd just been paid, and hadn't paid my bills yet. I thought long and deeply about what the money would mean to her life. I was already in financial difficulties, so if I sent her the money it would just mean struggling a bit more, for a bit longer… but what about my responsibilities, my family? After agonizing all day, I didn't send the money. Only a few weeks later I read in the paper that she'd died.

To this day I consider the consequences of my inability to make a contribution where it was needed. I couldn't help the world, but I could have made a difference to her. I realize that it was only because I was still in my NonSelf and wasn't producing the income to help her. I wasn't living out the true meaning and blessing of my creation, and so someone else suffered. This isn't meant to make anyone feel guilty. I'm sharing this story simply because it made *me* realize how important it is to be me, because of the huge difference that I make in the lives of others when I do *me*. My Journey has taken me to a place where, a few years ago, I set up The Man in the Mirror Foundation to help the needy, sick, and homeless. My shift now enables me to help others and contribute financially in a way that I could only have dreamed of a decade or so ago.

Insecurity and lack of courage meant I always used to try to fit in. I was rarely myself and did my psyche great harm by not being me. When I met with clients I was the person I thought they wanted me to be. When I was out with certain friends I would be a certain way. At home I played the strong father and husband, even though I felt weak inside. At social and business events I was quiet, unable to portray the confident person that I wanted to be. I only have one head but I wore so many different hats.

Many people, you included, may think that you have to be different things to different people. It's not true. The absolute best person to be is 'You.' Discover who you are and just be that person in all contexts, no pretense required.

More educators should spend time helping young adults discover who they are and give them the courage to say, do, and be themselves. If this were the case, I truly believe that there would be more happy and confident 40–50-year-olds. We would all be happier, more confident, and relaxed, that's for sure. You can't be nervous when you're just 'You.' The pain of my 20s and early 30s meant I learned about me and I had the courage to be what I learned. I do a great 'me' now.

🕐 *Whatever I do in life, I only do me now.*

Fear of what others around you think, do, or say is a sure reason for failure in ordinary men and women. They stay ordinary because they seem to care more about what others think of them than why they are here and the expression of their own unique existence. It's sometimes only on their deathbeds that they accept and realize how they've failed to live life as they wanted to, as they were on the inside; and then they slip off to who knows where.

TWO MEMORABLE MEN

I remember June 25, 2009, for two people. No matter what your judgments about Michael Jackson, you have to admit he gave it everything in the few decades of his life. Whatever gifts, talents, and genius creation were in him, Michael discovered it and gave those 'abilities' to the world. He found out what he was really made of, and spent his life getting that out into the world. Michael was meticulous in how he wanted things in his professional life. He kept to a Standard and quality of work and production that the next generations tried, and are still trying, to emulate. When he died, all of his music, his dance, his lyrics, his creations were out there in the world: Realize[2].

The other person I remember is Matthew Kelly, because I attended his funeral that day. He died aged 42. Matt wasn't an all-singing, all-dancing mega superstar; he was just himself, and he was my friend. Matt was only himself and people either took to him or they didn't, because he wasn't going to change and be false or not himself. Most people adored him, but everyone respected him because what you saw was what you got. Matt proved his friendship time and time again. He was also a very successful businessman and a great salesman. In a completely non-selfish way, Matt was a genius because he discovered who he was and was only ever himself: Realize². What percentage of people do you think can say that? Realize².

GET YOUR MUSIC OUT

Remember my friend Steve Olsher, who had a vision of his own eulogy as he held his dying stepfather's hand? What do *you* think people will say about you? What will be your self-eulogy?

How often have you heard the metaphor, 'Don't die with your music still in you'? What does it really mean to you? Did you change when you heard those words? Did you have a revelation, like Dickens's Scrooge in *A Christmas Carol*? Or did it just tickle your interest for a second before you let it go and got on with your life? Consider those words again. Pause a while and let the words translate into thoughts, ideas, and feelings. This is your life after all, and when you do what you love you really never classify it as work do you?

LAST STORIES

Judy Wright is a life and family coach, and a best-selling author. She now spends part of her time helping others to bounce back from life's challenges. An earlier part of her life was spent with the dying. As a result of that work she experienced many of what she calls 'end-of-life stories.' In that time Judy found three common regrets of the dying:

They wished they had risked more.

They felt they should have reflected more.

They wished they had contributed more and been more of a part of their own lives.

Imagine you're lying on your deathbed, looking around the room. As your eyes scan slowly around, you look at your loved ones. These are your family and friends. They are with you in your final moments as you reflect upon your life – the life you lived, and the life you could have lived. Do you want to be remembered for all your unsung music? Or for having all of your 'music' out there in the world? Dancing, moving, affecting, and singing in the lives of the people that you met – the energy of your inner child out there playing – playing even in the lives of people that you never met, who had their lives positively affected by you having lived? You shared your great TrueSelf and made a difference in their lives. Your music lives on because you walked a Journey of discovery to the true you, and you gave your TrueSelf to this world.

🕐 *When will you get the music that is inside of you outside of you?*

JUST GET STARTED

What would it mean to you, knowing that you had lived a happy, successful, and fulfilling life? I ask because I'm in no doubt that had the good Lord called me just a few years ago, my life was so unfulfilled that if it weren't for my family, it would have been viewed as an unremarkable life: one more life for the 'wasted and unrealized potential' epitaph pile. As the American author Napoleon Hill said, 'No one is richer than the person who has found their labor of love and is busily engaged in performing it.' This is another way of saying realize what you are and spend your life making that real: Realize².

We don't know the hour we'll be called from this place, so why do we act as if we do? When all of your gifts, talents, words of comfort, potential, abilities, smiles, and acts of love are out there, this is what it means to have truly shared, to have lived. When it's your time to move on, you'll want to know that you enjoyed the Journey as You because you realized the real You and your talents: Realize². This is what it means to have known the Truth and to have lived your life as your TrueSelf. Why do we only comprehend these things when it's too late to do something about it?

> 🕐 **Excuses don't pay the bills. Happiness needs no excuses.**

I've spent over a quarter of a century meeting people every day and finding out what makes them tick, what they really want in life, and what's most important to them. They have shared what they think makes them happy. One of the things I learned is that most people are as happy as they make up their minds to be, no matter what happens, and that is their chosen Standard of existence. For some, happiness is not something they experience 'in the present moment,' it happens at some point in the future when they will have this, do that, or be something else.

A common complaint of some of my coaching clients is that they feel pushed and pulled, or floating along in life. But the turning point toward success and happiness for many people who felt they were 'failures' came at a moment when they were caused, forced, or chose to be ultra-honest with themselves and realized they'd just had 'enough' of that problem, or way of life, and decided to change as a result of being in that moment. For these people that's all it took. In the majority of cases the moment was the catalyst to unleashing their inner powers, gifts, and abilities.

0–10 YOUR MOMENTS

Be conscious of your instincts, feelings, and intuition. Nurture and encourage these seeds of your inner self as they respond to your call. Use these communications to get a clearer feel and vision of who you are and what you are here for. In holding that space you'll begin to exist more as the real you, with all your potential power coming through. When in your TrueSelf, ask the best way to make real whatever you realize is inside of you. How do you do this? By paying attention to, then following, the words, thoughts, question, phrases, and ideas that come from your TrueSelf. Your TrueSelf will do the rest the more you allow it to.

WHAT DID YOU SAY YOU WERE WAITING FOR?

Many people wait to take action, to speak certain words, to share love, but that is all they do, wait. They wait as if they have time to stop putting off until tomorrow what they should have done yesterday. These people live as if they have a guarantee of plenty of time to wake up and begin to realize who and what they are in the world.

My mother died when she was only 36 years old. I don't know what goals, dreams, and plans she had. I knew her only as many of us know our nearest and dearest, in love. Unbeknown to her, her physical time on this Earth was short-lived. Her eternal spirit had its time here, completed its role in its physical form and is now somewhere else. Life is short; when are you going to live it?

PARABLE OF THE TALENTS

A wealthy landowner went on sabbatical. He wondered what to do with his cash and decided to leave it in the care of his three honest servants. He left five talents to one servant, two talents to the next, and one talent to a third. When he returned he gathered his servants together and asked for the return of this money and whatever gains the servants had made while it was in their care.

The first servant proudly explained how he had bought and sold at market until he had doubled the money. The second servant eagerly told how he had put the money to work with the local merchants to make a profit. The master was pleased and gave both men a promotion. But the last servant said nothing, he simply returned the one talent, saying, 'Master, I was afraid to use the talent in case I lost it, so I buried it deep in the ground, marking the spot where I left it carefully, and now I return to you what I was given.'

The master was angry and replied, 'I gave you a talent and you did nothing with it. Leave my land… even that little which you had, if unused, will be taken away from you.'

🕐 **Within you is the change that you have been waiting for.**

Now is the time to act, to think, to love, to change. The past doesn't matter for there's no past you can buy or re-inherit. There's no future except the 'now' that you created in the past. When you get to the future, all you have is another now. And it is only the now that you can make use of. All we ever have is more now. Each of us is here to live to realize what is within us, and to realize our gifts and talents in the world: Realize^2. If this weren't true, we wouldn't be here on Earth with them.

My TrueSelf told me that if I set new, higher Standards for how I lived and as myself, then my life would never be the same again and that I would live my real life: The life I deserve and the one I came here for. My TrueSelf told me that if I set Standards for all of my life then somehow

I would get to know my TrueSelf better and better as I went along my path. I followed my intuition and that has made all the difference. If you never find out who you really are, and get that person out into the world, how can you be happy? And as the great motivational speaker Les Brown said, 'And if you can't be happy, then what else is there?'

0–10 YOUR MOMENTS

This is a little exercise in knowing you. Write down the answers to the following questions:

1. What is it that you always wanted to do?
2. What are you secretly passionate about?
3. What did you yearn to accomplish?
4. What did you excel at or love, but give up?
5. Where do you feel you can you make the biggest positive difference?
6. What do you really enjoy doing the most?
7. What's your gut feeling about your purpose?
8. Who do you feel you really are?

To excel in your discovery of your higher truer self, ask these questions every day: in the morning when you get up and before you go to sleep. Keep these words by your bedside and carry out this simple exercise of asking and honestly answering these questions for as many days as it takes to get the answers burning inside you. Then the fire will feed you as you fed it.

The journey within is greater than any journey in the wide world.

THE JOY OF TRUESELF

When I found my TrueSelf, things changed in every area of my life. I began to understand Gerry and our children more. We were able to reenergize our relationship because I had changed. Our disjointed family relationships made their way back to wholeness. Gerry and I found greater happiness and were comfortable with the change. I knew my Truth and that everything else would be okay. In the process I was able to set new Standards for my life and found another way to do the same business. This new way was easy and effective. I became more patient with my children, accepting the absent parent I had been. It's curious, but when I changed, the people closest to me and others became nicer people, too! I was able to see them as they really were – in light. I knew how I'd been with my family and closest friends, and realizing they loved me both before and after I truly found myself I became centered in my TrueSelf, accepting how those around me would react to the true me.

It is a joyous thing to take true responsibility for yourself and your life. As you become your TrueSelf and take responsibility for being yourself, you too will find joy in the difference. Find your TrueSelf and live only as you from now on, while knowing your Realize[2] is all about discovering you, and being you in the service and facilitation of others. Love of others will get you all that you want for yourself. In the extraordinary financial times that we live in, you need to be all you can be to make it in this world. Realize² in love of others will get you all that you want for yourself: happiness and success.

ONE OF MY PRESENT 'MOMENTS'

I had some great news earlier this year when I heard that *Of Mary*, directed by Adrian Lester, had won 'Best Short Film' at the PAFF 2012 awards. The film's Director of Photography was Luke Redgrave of the Redgrave acting dynasty, who has worked on many major movies. *Of Mary* had already won the accolade of being screened at Europe's largest independent film festival, Raindance. My pleasure comes because I was the Executive Producer for the film, as a result of being in my TrueSelf and following my inspired intuition of a 10-second moment.

A couple of years ago I was approached by my friend Ruth Needham to meet with Adrian Lester, Lolita Chakrabarti, and Rosa Maggiora, who run a film production company. Ruth mentioned they needed to find the right person to work with. For them it wasn't just about the money, it was about the connection and the synergy, and Ruth told me that my presence immediately came to her in that moment and she announced to them, 'I know just the person.' At the time she didn't know of my longstanding creative interest in film, or that I had discussed a couple of ideas with a movie producer in Los Angeles a few years earlier. Both ideas are still very much alive.

When I met Adrian and the team at BAFTA in London, we discussed our backgrounds and our philosophies, and as I sat there I knew it was the right thing to do. They didn't know it then, but it took just a few moments into our first meeting for me to realize that they were the right people for me to start my film production career. My gut feeling gave me the message that it was right. *Of Mary* was our first production, and more are planned.

Every day now, when I'm in the flow of TrueSelf, triggers are everywhere. I experience my moments and want to share whatever's inside me at that moment.

The core of the 10-Second Philosophy is the existence of a greater you within – a truer you that is connected to everything of which you are also a part. Traveling your Journey to TrueSelf and living your Truth simultaneously allows you access to your Faculty, and via Conduit, collaboration with intelligent energy: the stuff that is and permeates you, me, the universe, and everything. The universe conspires for good.

Think about it…

'Is there anything that can stop the ripples of a stone thrown in a lake?'

You might answer, 'No, apart from the lake's shores, which are its physical limits.'

But the real answer is 'Yes, a larger stone!' The combined effect is that both ripples deviate and change direction to a lesser or greater degree, but the overall initial direction stops when a large enough stone is thrown in the lake. Then the original forces at work in that lake are permanently changed. Take this philosophy and make it your larger stone.

0–10 YOUR MOMENTS
· ·

There are many things that make us happy. It's different for all of us, but we know it when we see it. Think about it now: What does happiness mean to you and do you know it when you see it? With this you can Realize[2] and Be All You Can Be. Begin.

🕐 *This is the genesis of you.*

Contemplations on The 10-Second Philosophy®

We conclude where we began, by recognizing that there's 'something' inside – in you, in me, and everyone – an inner genius that, when aroused, will take you on an incredible Journey of realizations and success. With all of this comes happiness. For maybe the first time in your life you're in the place where it all began, within you. On my Journey I found my TrueSelf and learned I'm my own Guru. You are your own Guru. The answers are inside your TrueSelf, and what's inside of you connects you to the storehouse of wisdom and to everything else. The world gives too much credit to the conscious, logical, 'left-brain' mind. Much of this same society inwardly knows that there is 'something' else – an inner something and a greater something – but because it can't be weighed or measured, society relies on the 'rational mind' almost exclusively.

You may have reached for this book to create a better future, only to learn that a better future is based on what you do today and that you only ever have 'nows.' Nothing else exists. If you want to live in an incredible future of 'nows,' begin to live as your TrueSelf and at your Standards today, just for today, one day at a time. Standards aren't about being perfect, or better than anyone else, they're about being your best 'You' to serve, the best 'You' around others, and getting the best out of 'You' for yourself and others. Use your nows.

🕐 *Everything affects everything.*

SHAPING YOUR WORLD

Be unrealistically realistic. Think like the greats of the past by ignoring the realistic measure of things. It's wise and realistic to be unrealistic, and history has demonstrated this time and again, as those who shaped the world did it with their genius against the noise of the crowd. You may not directly be able to control what the rest of the world does, but daily adherence to your Standards will make an impact on everything you do immediately, and start to shape your world.

When you capture and internalize your 10-second moments you'll experience a shift in your life. It's the combination of your shifts that create your new reality. If, in that 10-second moment, you accept the shift, you'll have made a different decision from that intuitive place. As a result the universe will change positively for you, because in 'those' moments you take on your true mantle of co-creation. Even if you can't see the precise 'result' immediately, it will be there as a cause set in motion. The world that we live in today is based upon lots of these moments.

As you step into your TrueSelf and your life begins to change, I trust that one day you will share your story with me, so that I can continue to realize and help others. Thank you in anticipation of that. If you can live day by day to your TrueSelf Standards, you will have the best in your life. Let go of any attachment to the outcome or results. Simply be your Standards by the day and you'll find that the universe collaborates just fine for you. Your Journey can't be planned, even in your imagination, but with its magical twists and turns, it will exceed your expectations. Your Journey, like mine, is the constant and never-ending realization of your TrueSelf.

Whatever, in some wistful vision, you dreamed you are, as TrueSelf you are always, in all ways, more than that. How else could a child of immigrants with a stutter, who became near-depressed and broke and stayed just above broke for almost two decades, suddenly 'wake up;' discover his true genius and the treasures in the universe around him; and become an international speaker, coach, mentor, multi-millionaire, executive film producer, author, and wealth manager? What is the full extent of your human potential and purpose?

🕐 *We're not defined by the 'things' that*
happen to us, but by what we make of them.

YOU ARE THE CAUSE OR THE EFFECT

We live in a 'cause' and 'effect' world. You create at cause or you regret at effect. You choose. Living at *cause* is acting from your TrueSelf, living by your PERFECT Standards, accessing your Faculty and inner genius, and accepting that you have resourceful options. Living at effect is living according to Standards imposed on you, reacting instead of operating from your core, and as a result, your TrueSelf becomes quieter. Living at cause, you take responsibility and have the life you want because you create your world as you go along. You choose to live from a place of Realize[2].

THE MOUNTAIN

There is a mountain, a spiritual mountain, that exists. The mountain is near the source. Some people choose to live on the mountain, benefitting from its strength, breathing its air, and cleansing constantly the burdens of the world. Others choose to live away from the mountain. Some of those people don't know that there is a mountain and some don't care for it, while others know that it's there but struggle to find time in their lives to move toward it.

In my talks and coaching I regularly meet OnMo (on-the-mountain) and OffMo (off-the-mountain) people. OnMo people are often the nicest, kindest, most spiritual people you could hope to meet. Some occupy base camp and others are near the top, meditating and praying for you, the world and me, but Mother Teresa they are not. Mother Teresa, as saintly as she was, knew the importance of money in this world. She demonstrated this when she used it to help the poor and sick. It saddens me when I meet lovely, spiritual people who are struggling to pay the bills, and my intention is in helping them to realize that they too could have the financial benefits of the world if that's what they want.

OffMo people occupy the material world. The extreme OffMo people believe it's about the money. The extreme OffMo people live far from the mountain. It's still their mountain, but if it doesn't fold and they can't count it, it doesn't matter to them. It is also my intention that my work helps OffMo people to benefit and have a richer experience of the world, being true to themselves while still making money and enjoying their Journey.

It's also my desire to help people who view themselves in any way OffMo to move toward and even onto the mountain. It will be my bliss to see this happen and for the world to benefit as a result. I understand now that the path leading from the mountain and the path leading to the mountain are the same path. What matters is what direction you're going. Which direction are you going? What do you feel is inside of you now?

We live in a construct of the collective consciousness of the NonSelf OffMo people and TrueSelf OnMo people. Everything that keeps you away from TrueSelf, keeps you off the mountain. Sometimes it may feel easier to stay away from the mountain, to stay asleep. But that feeling is nothing more than another hook or trap of NonSelf. That feeling is nothing but an illusion.

When you begin to act from inner sapience, some people whom you have known for years will begin to 'see' you for the very first time. Some, who have been on the periphery of your life and living mutually 'unseen' for a very long time, will begin to 'see' you. The cognoscenti of your client and business world will 'see' you too, and treat you accordingly. And those otherwise connected 'strangers' you meet will see you now, too. As you change along your Journey, others change, too, reflecting your new self back at you. The right clients, friends, and connections will find you; the 'wrong' ones won't. Don't let your fear of what people may say about you kill your ability to access your TrueSelf abilities. Painful experience has taught me that living your life as the world expects is harder than attempting to run with lead boots and a bungee band on.

⏱ *Is that (really) you?*

WHY THIS PHILOSOPHY NOW?

Someone once said, 'You can be the fountain or you can be the drain.' With so many not achieving goals, living less happy and failing lives, there is a need for a paradigm shift. How can we know so much more as a species, yet have the same fears and contradictions, insecurities, and failings as before? I know that we face challenges and I'm confident that we will always change and rise to them. I decided to write this book now because I felt deep down that it was important to do so at this time. I was led by my TrueSelf, my core, and my intuition.

Our eldest daughter Rochelle said recently, 'Magic moments are when things just come to your mind.' The

10-Second Philosophy title came to me while I ruminated in my TrueSelf, sitting on a bed in Tipperary, Ireland. I was considering how to best share my philosophy with a wider audience. It was a 'magic moment.'

It may seem strange that a less-than-ordinary guy just changed, became happy, began to ruminate on the purpose of his life and life itself, and impacted people around the globe. Any time we are ready, we can wake up to our inner genius. Age is not a factor. The Italian tenor Andrea Bocelli studied law until he was in his 30s and then became an opera singer. J.K. Rowling wanted to write and Harry Potter was her Realize[2]. Delia Smith, the UK's best-selling cookery author of over 21 million books, always wanted to cook. Aged 16 she studied and washed dishes in a restaurant. As she washed, she paid attention to what was going on inside her and discovered practical ways of cooking that would make it easier for others. She dropped out of structured education, and the rest is history. Each of these people, and many more throughout the world and history, was on one track and completely changed once they found themselves.

🕐 *Glad that I found you.*

YOU CAN'T FAIL AS YOUR TRUESELF

I'm sometimes asked, 'What if I fail, what then?' Whenever you're stuck in treacle it's not failure, it's knowledge, and it tells you that you're not in your TrueSelf space enough. You can never fail as your TrueSelf, you can only learn and experience, and learn to trust the meaning of this apparent 'failure.' It will reveal itself to you soon, and later will have multiple meanings. Instead of beating yourself up, begin to say, 'I know what I did with my life and I'm pleased with it because it has led me here.'

I cannot take back the early steps of my Journey, my failure in my 20s and 30s, and my early reluctance as a 'guru,' nor would I want to. For if I hadn't taken those early steps, I wouldn't have found the light of life. I continue to realize my TrueSelf today, and follow what comes to and through me and share it and myself with others because I know that is my Realize[2].

The Moving Finger writes; and, having writ,
Moves on: nor all thy Piety nor Wit
Shall lure it back to cancel half a Line,
Nor all thy tears wash out a Word of it.
OMAR KHAYYÁM, PERSIAN POLYMATH

May you continue to understand who and what you are and have the courage to make that real. By now, you may be blessed to have already begun to recognize your TrueSelf and your realization. May you continue to grasp the importance of appreciating your TrueSelf as you continue to stir, to become conscious and to awake, and to take your hero or heroine's Journey.

Whatever dwells in your head now will change as you shift to your heart and intuition. Go there and ask, 'Who am I and where have I been?' You'll quickly realize that you're an intelligent being in a body, so just find out who you are and then be only that. Trying to be anything else is a blueprint for disaster.

My Journey continues today, and along the way I hear many people saying, 'Oh this is meant to be,' as if there was some huge interstellar diagram of how things are meant to happen. We're not clockwork mice running through some predetermined maze. We came into these physical bodies to *experience* and to *express*. Some people use 'meant to be' almost as an excuse for what happens to them. I don't believe this, but I do feel that we can give meaning to anything we choose. 'There's not much good or bad, but thinking makes it so,' as Shakespeare tells us in *Hamlet*. There is no divine blueprint because we are all connected but independent energy, souls in physical bodies, so we have choices (some more than others). We can choose to be responsible and take charge of our lives, being the 'something' that is in us all. We can all take action based on our questions to self and guidance from within.

I believe that the 'something' people saw in me as my life changed was nothing more or less than an open spirit shining. It was and remains an outward expression of the inner wonder, possibility, and connectedness within us all: The Faculty and the Conduit to everything else.

GO, BONNIE!

A doctor friend of mine, Bonnie, is a medical practice manager who uses her TrueSelf to guide her life and career. She once shared how she uses her TrueSelf inner voice and feelings like radar to guide her. This is rather like the 'hot and cold' game you might have played as a child (where you're given hints and clues as you move closer or further away from the thing you're trying to find). In the same way, Bonnie allows her TrueSelf intuition to move her toward or away from people, jobs, and opportunities, and trusts that it won't let her down. And it doesn't. She says, 'Listening to my intuition is definitely the *key* to my life right now... I have faith it will lead me in the right direction and help the right opportunities to manifest at the right time. However, it does take faith.' She e-mailed me recently to tell me that she had been offered a job in Massachusetts: 'To call it my dream job would be an understatement!' Her Journey has taken her to a place where she can live and play out her inner genius. You can tell that she's happy and shining now, can't you? Go, Bonnie!

When you trust yourself, you too will have your own way of knowing what is better or worse for you.

A PRACTICAL PHILOSOPHY

You wouldn't eat a teaspoon of salt, a cup of sugar, flour, or two raw eggs. That makes no sense to me, but mixed together and baked for long enough, at the right temperature, you have a beautiful cake. The 10-Second Philosophy is a practical philosophy, so take it as such. Stir together the different ingredients to make your world better for it. Individual parts of the philosophy are somewhat like that cake. They are okay on their own, but in the right context, mixed with the other ingredients of the philosophy and used for long enough with the right attitude, they will make you a lovelier life. You will become what you really are when you Realize[2] what you can be.

If you have a strong enough 'why' we're told, you can endure or find the 'how' of success. Is this true for everyone? I don't think so. What if your 'why' is strong, but you can't find the 'how'? What if you are 97 years old and the 'how' never came to you? It is my deepest self-realization that somewhere, somehow, through use of this philosophy, that you find a 'how.'

• You know that as TrueSelf you're in your core, centered space, so you can use your intuitions and inner guidance. Through your Standards you get to live each day as you.

• You know to play with and trust the Law of Connection. If you haven't taken charge of your heart and mind for a while, now you can and will live each day as you. Now is your time to bring your own world to life by realizing what is inside of you and what you are capable of in making those gifts real in the world. Now is your time.

• You know that this whole philosophy is designed to give you gateways to your TrueSelf and keep you in that space longer. You know that there are many gateways to TrueSelf. You know now that in mere seconds, about 10 seconds, you can step through a gateway and touch the real 'You.'

• You know that contentment and peace of mind will be some of the first shifts that will occur in your life in TrueSelf. This is a material world, so financial wealth will be obvious and enduring. I urge you to trust your TrueSelf; you don't have to force any issues or stress on yourself to make things happen. If you are, then you're not doing '*You*' right.

- You know that my life became my own once I stepped onto the 'happy and success elevator' of TrueSelf, and began to ride it onward and upward. Even though you wouldn't have witnessed any more money in my bank account in those few seconds, I began to live joyfully, as if I had the life I had dreamed of, because from that moment I did. You can immediately begin to celebrate life. Live it as well as you can, in the service of others, and you will enjoy a greater Journey as you watch what flows.

- You know we are connected, so we have met and will again.

- Most of all, you know that you can only be truly happy as your TrueSelf.

> ⏱ *You are the success that you seek.*

THE 10-SECOND PHILOSOPHY®

We come now to the final and most important exercise of this book.

You know that a word, thought, question, phrase, or idea can, if you allow it, take you inside to find and access the characteristics of your TrueSelf. Once you have read to the end of the book, take time to go through the book again. Only this time go immediately back to the beginning and read only the 10-second statements identified by the ⏱ symbol. Use these statements to guide you and create a 'moment' for you.

Pause. Take a moment with each statement. Read each one and give it at least 10 seconds internal pondering before moving on to the next. This is not a time to flick through or rush. This is a time to sit quietly and consider. Let each statement sink into you as you consider its effect, impact, or potential for you. Invest the time to do this now and the future will bring you rewards and self-knowledge. In doing so you will be releasing your inner genius.

This is how you use the 10-Second Philosophy.

YOUR MOMENT BEGINS

From this moment, pay attention and be watchful. Success looks different to each individual. My success is unique to me as a result of following a philosophy and a process. If you find that any part of this philosophy resonates with you, put it into practice for yourself today.

Some follow the path worn and set out by others. You can create your own path, based upon your discovery of who you really are, your TrueSelf, because the self-revelation reveals the genius of who you really are.

Success and happiness won't be achieved by waiting for some other book or some other meeting or for some other time. It will not be yours if you wait for another person.

Within you is what you have been waiting for. Within you is what you seek. It's you.

I believe that success and happiness in life is based upon a 10-Second Philosophy. Once you've accepted the right word, thought, question, phrase, or idea, and allowed it to lead you to your TrueSelf, which is your inner genius, then you will be more powerful than you previously dared to realize. You will discover parts of yourself you didn't know, and make a positive difference not just to your immediate surroundings, but to your broader world at large.

Be in the 10-second moments that appear for you. Begin to begin.

Connect with Derek:
- www.derek-mills.com
- info@derekmills.co.uk
- www.facebook.com/DerekMills.StandardsGuy
- www.twitter.com/derekmills1

ABOUT THE AUTHOR

The son of Jamaican immigrants, **Derek Mills** was born in Birmingham, England. He grew up happily with his six brothers and sisters until, when he was 13, his mother unexpectedly died. This affected Derek deeply and he developed a severe stutter.

Everything was on a downward spiral in Derek's life – his work, his physical and mental health, and his relationships with family and friends. It only took one insignificant question from an office security guard one night for Derek to stop, connect deep within himself, and in the next 10 seconds begin to see a way to change his entire life completely.

He turned his life and business around, creating balance and harmony, and becoming a millionaire businessman in three years. As he began to develop and share his methodology – The 10-Second Philosophy® – in front of international audiences, he was invited to coach and mentor others. This unique philosophy and his PERFECT Life Standards System™ have made even some of the best coaches, consultants, and speakers in the world stop and reconsider the concept of goal setting.

By invitation he is a Fellow of the British-American Project, an organization that exists to develop relationships between perceived future leaders in Britain and the USA. He is a featured expert in the personal development movie *The Keeper of the Keys*, and executive producer on the award-winning film short *Of Mary*. Derek is also a Senior Partner in one of the UK's premier Wealth Management organizations.

Derek is passionate about helping people all over the world to make the changes that transforms their lives. He regularly speaks to audiences of over 7,000 people.

www.derek-mills.com